OCT   1993

OCT   1993

T H E
FIFTIES
A PICTORIAL REVIEW

*To Auntie Sylvia and
Uncle Maurice*

T H E
FIFTIES

A PICTORIAL REVIEW

To Auntie Sylvia and
Uncle Maurice

THE FIFTIES

A PICTORIAL REVIEW

Chris Pearce

Perma·lift
GIRDLES
BRASSIERES

Pert and perky is this wispy lit
"Perma-lift" Pantie—fabulous
dainty, yet marvelously stron
So comfortable too, and N
Bones About It—Stays l
Without Stays—the Magic Ins
eliminates annoying bones, y
it can't roll over, wrinkle
bind. Get yours at your favor
corsetiere's today, or write f
name of nearest deal

Power Net Pantie $6.95 White or Pi
Sizes 24 to 30
Power Net Girdle $5.95 White or Pi
Sizes 24 to 30

BLOSSOM

An H. C. Blossom Book

A catalogue record for this book is available from the British Library

ISBN 1 872532 26 8

Design: Jacquie Burgess and Ivor Claydon

Typeset in Great Britain by SX Composing, Rayleigh, Essex.

Printed and bound in Hong Kong

H. C. Blossom
6/7 Warren Mews
London W1P 5DJ

CONTENTS

INTRODUCTION

The fifties was the age of the 'hard sell'. This was aggressive marketing unfettered by consumer rights legislation, the morality of which only became questioned towards the end of the decade. Improvements in colour printing had been responsible for an increased number of magazines to carry the message of consumerism as well as a profusion of eye-catching packaging. More significantly, television became a major vehicle not only for marketing products but also 'selling politics,' as well as influencing the popular arts and social behaviour.

The success of this marketing can be measured by the continuing effect it has on our current popular concept of the era, which is predominantly one of glamour and excitement, kept alive by new generations coming under the spell. Ironically, the age which introduced planned obsolesence as an essential part of its marketing strategy has in many ways left some of the most enduring images of this century. So much of the fifties is still finding appeal it is worth remembering that the decade ended thirty years ago, and that many who have an affection for the period — be it in the images of Marilyn Monroe and James Dean, cars, fashion and furniture, rock 'n' roll music or just a general romanticized nostalgia — were not even born at that time.

The intervening years have brought so much change that it has to be pointed out that during the fifties Japan was only just beginning to be seen as an international industrial force, that for nearly all the time East-West ideological conflict dominated world politics, that electronics featured but little in home and workplace, and that international travel was still a novelty.

The inheritance of the forties was not a happy one. Not only were the scars of World War II very much in evidence — in Europe with devastated cities and economies only just starting to be re-built, — and in the United States with post war recession and social unrest — but international tension was threatening a return to global conflict. The last months of the forties had seen Mao Tse Tung's revolution culminate in China becoming a communist republic, the East-West division of Germany, the Soviet Union testing its first atomic bomb, and the growing anti-communist movement within the USA.

Tension between Russia and America, the main antagonists in the conflict of ideologies, and the attendant threat of atomic war provided the backdrop against which the events of the age were played. One effect which this had on America and, through its influence, the Western world, was the political (as well as economic) doctrine

Key to a richer life

This is Main Street, U. S. A. It is unlike any other Main Street anywhere else in the world.

It is rich in contentment and well-being. It bustles with hearty and wholesome activity. And as you see and know firsthand, it revolves very largely around the family car.

Along every Main Street in America, General Motors cars are a of consumerism. Simply, the acquisitive society came to symbolise Western values, and not to participate fully in it was regarded as unpatriotic, even subversive. In 1956 President Eisenhower prescribed consumer spending as the cure for the recession that threatened the bonanza trail of conspicuous consumption on which the economy was founded, and, it was only towards the end of the decade that any failure to subscribe to these values could occur without being regarded as seditious.

By the time Vance Packard and Ralph Nader challenged the power of the Corporations they were only articulating a generally felt disenchantment, but until then only the wierdo beat poets and harrassed breadwinners on the treadmill of finance repayments questioned the ordained order. Just as consumerism became the nucleus of Western society, by the same token Communism, or anything which could possibly be interpreted as tainted with it, was regarded as dangerous. Although this polarisation of values was at its most extreme in America, the effects were also felt in Europe and had a profound influence upon the whole decade.

Left *The car became the ultimate symbol of the affluent society, so that in 1950 when General Motors was promising 'a richer life' most consumers would have taken it literally – the fulfilment of materialism.*

Right *The sinister side of technology cast its shadow over the decade in the form of the mushroom cloud, which became a familiar* memento mori *as atomic bomb tests were carried out.*

DEDICATED TO AMERICA'S DEFENSE

GENERAL ⊕ ELECTRIC

CHAPTER ONE
REDS UNDER THE BED
AND SENATOR McCARTHY

In 1947 President Harry Truman announced a policy to counter communism on a global scale. Fearing that the poverty and social unrest of post-war Europe made it vulnerable to communism, the United States introduced the Marshall Plan, named after Secretary of State George Marshall. Seventeen billion dollars worth of food, raw materials and the industrial plant and tools needed to rebuild industry was sent into Western Europe, prompting Russia to complain of 'dollar imperialism', and pressurizing Finland and Czechoslovakia into refusing assistance.

Anti-communist hysteria was also building up in America, fuelled by strikes and post-war social unrest, economic recession and the beginnings of what would become the civil rights movement. The communications industry was considered a breeding ground for subversion. The Federal Communications Commission, which regulated broadcasting and telephone companies, received the unsolicited intervention of J. Edgar Hoover when it began to assess the suitability of applicants for television broadcasting licences. Although unsubstantiated, Hoover's claim that 'the majority of these individuals are members of the Communist Party or have affiliated themselves sympathetically with the activities of the Communist movement effectively influenced the Commission's activities. Rather than offend him, they agreed to accept his 'guidance'.

Right *America saw itself under threat from Communism in the form of subversion (which Senator McCarthy was rooting out) and militarism. In 1952 General Electric advertised their contribution to the nation's defence in popular magazines* (**Left**).

BEYOND
CASABLANCA
in Damascus...
Destiny,
in a low-cut
gown,
lies in wait
for
BOGART

COLUMBIA PICTURES presents

HUMPHREY
BOGART
in
Sirocco

co-starring

MARTA TOREN · LEE J. COBB

WITH
EVERETT SLOANE · GERALD MOHR · ZERO MOSTEL

Screen Play by A. I. BEZZERIDES and HANS JACOBY · Based upon the novel,
"Coup de Grace", by Joseph Kessel · A SANTANA PRODUCTION
Produced by ROBERT LORD · Directed by CURTIS BERNHARDT

..Meet terrific new
ar find...torrid

Left *Humphrey Bogart was one of several big-name stars who fought the anti-communist hysteria which swept through Hollywood.*

Unable to resist the anti-communist panic, Truman authorized Executive Order no. 9835 under which two and a half million federal employees would be checked by 'loyalty review boards', who would act on information from the FBI and others. The Attorney General supplied a list of 'subversive' organizations. Although the order was limited to federal employees, the House Committee on Un-American Activities, whose membership included an ambitious young lawyer, Richard M. Nixon, began its investigation of communism within the film industry.

Jack Warner testified that screen writers were subversives, and the level of hysteria rose so far that the mother of the film star Ginger Rogers testified that the film *None but the Lonely Heart* was pro-communist, citing as evidence a review which described it as 'moody and sombre throughout, in the Russian manner'. As the witchhunt started, the Chairman of the Committee claimed to have evidence against seventy-nine Hollywood communists. The President of the Screen Actors Guild, Ronald Reagan, made a dignified appeal: 'I hope that we are never prompted by fear or resentment of communism into compromising any of our democratic principles in order to fight them.' Hollywood divided into those who valued their integrity and those who went with the tide.

Major stars, including Humphrey Bogart and Gene Kelly, protested against the proceedings. Ten major screen writers were blacklisted for refusing to recognize the Committee or answer its questions, and were subsequently imprisoned for contempt of Congress despite having invoked the Fifth Amendment. A private organization, American Business Consultants, run by three former FBI agents, began publishing *Counterattack, the Newsletter of Facts on Communism*. It's most influential publication was *Red Channels: Communist Influence in Radio and Television*, which listed 151 subversives, including Larry Adler, Leonard Bernstein, Aaron Copeland, Burl Ives, Artie Shaw, Gypsy Rose Lee, Arthur Miller and Orson Welles.

Left *Ronald Reagan's stance against the Hollywood witch-hunt was a courageous act at a time when the merest hint of Communist sympathies could mean the end of a professional career.*

The fate of intellectuals was not considered of public importance, despite the occasional suicide, but the alarm bells started ringing when the name Lucille Ball appeared as a subversive. The star of the *I Love Lucy* TV Show, America's Favourite, it turned out, had in fact joined the Communist Party in 1936. Although others were being pilloried on less substantial evidence, it was unthinkable that any harm should befall Lucy, and the matter was quickly explained away when it was revealed that though it was true she had joined the CP, this was only the innocent action of a dutiful young girl who had enrolled at the request of her grandfather whose happiness had been her only thought!

America was suffering from a collective paranoia which was to gag or reduce the influence of the liberals and intellectuals who may otherwise have been able to counteract some of the worst excesses of corporate power which were to characterize the fifties.

Anti-communist purges were not confined to America. In 1948 British Prime Minister Clement Attlee announced that known communists would be removed from security-sensitive positions in the Civil Service, and in fact some civil servants were suspended.

Above *Clement Attlee was at one stage branded a Communist by McCarthy, despite having instigated a purge of the British Civil Service.*

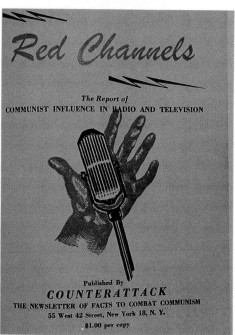

Left *Commercial sponsors and advertisers were obliged to consult the Red Channels blacklist to ensure that they would not be tarnished by association with programmes involving alleged Communist sympathisers.*

Right *Even though the anti-communist witch-hunt was destroying reputations and ruining lives, it was unthinkable that Lucille Ball, the epitome of American young motherhood, should be branded a Commie. The excuse she gave for having joined the Communist Party was taken as a pardonable justification.*

Lucille Ball, as photographed by Mead-Maddick, on the set of "I Love Lucy" (Monday Nights, CBS-TV

"I love telegrams," says Lucy—"especially Bunnygrams!"

Television's one and only Lucy is reading a Bunnygram to little Ricky. It's Western Union's special Easter greeting for children. Don't you know a child who would be as thrilled as Ricky to get his own Easter telegram, signed by Peter Rabbit himself? Of course you do! Call Western Union today!

And when you do, don't forget the grownups. Be sure to send *them* the Easter greeting that says so much . . . the *personal* message on Western Union's beautifully decorated Easter greeting blank. Share your joy with family and friends the most thoughtful way of all—Easter greetings by wire.

BUNNYGRAMS FOR CHILDREN...
EASTER WIRES FOR GROWNUPS!

BY WESTERN UNION

SINCE THE OUTBREAK of war in Korea, America has been working against time to build up its Air Power. Only our military leaders and Congress can decide how *much* Air Power we should have at any given time. Yet, as a leading manufacturer, we feel a responsibility to help you understand the vast complexity of modern aircraft . . . and why a "happy medium" level of production must be maintained in peace so that we can expand quickly to meet emergencies. Second-best Air Power is not enough in war. America's future security demands a long-range Air Power program in peace as well as in emergencies.

RADAR-GUIDED, NEAR-SONIC LOCKHEED F-94C INTERCEPTORS, POWERED BY MIGHTY PRATT & WHITNEY J-48 JET ENGINES, ARE ARMED WITH 48 AIR-TO-AIR ROCKETS.

Left *The public were constantly reassured that military technology was up to the task of defending the American Way of Life. This 1953 advertisement was for the United Aircraft Corporation.*

Above *Ten years later the issue was to dominate all others, yet when this picture appeared in 1955 few Americans were aware of their country's involvement in Vietnam.*

Ironically, in 1953 the ringmaster of America's anti-commuist hunt, McCarthy, would attack Attlee in a speech to the US Senate as 'Comrade Attlee', accusing him of treason and contributing to the expansion of communism. Attlee's addition to McCarthy's daily-increasing list of 'commies' and their friends is hardly justified, for despite the post-war Labour government's socialist programme, which emphasized nationalization and the Welfare State, his own party was criticizing him for not taking the programme far enough. In any event, Attlee had supported Truman's decision to back South Korea against the communist North Korean invasion in 1950 and, under the auspices of the United Nations sent British naval and military support.

In this manner, the decade began with the conflict of Communism and Capitalism being fought both on the battlefields of Korea and at home, within the corridors of power.

In the wake of ex-State Department official Alger Hiss's five-year prison sentence for perjury (he had originally been under investigation for spying for Russia), Senator McCarthy made his historic announcement that he had 'in his hand' a list of 'two hundred and fifty members of the Communist Party still working and shaping the policy of the State Department'.

Intoxicated by the resultant publicity, he called for the impeachment of President Truman, accusing Truman and Dean Acheson of being 'the Pied Pipers of the Politburo', as well as describing General George C. Marshall (who as Secretary of State had introduced the Marshall Plan to counteract communism and who had been Chief of the US General Staff during the war) as 'a man steeped in falsehood' and 'an instrument of the Soviet conspiracy'. He saw himself as the defender of Common America: 'McCarthyism is Americanism with its sleeve rolled'. Fear of his power to blight careers and topple reputations tainted a government powerless to halt the witchhunt.

It was hoped that Eisenhower's triumphant election to the presidency would put a stop to this destruction. Unfortunately, although it was the General's military skills which had appealed to the electorate who wanted a speedy end to the Korean War, he seemed powerless against McCarthy and would not confront him: "I refuse to get into the gutter with that guy." The *New York Herald Tribune* reported an aborted interview on the subject, in which Eisenhower, hands clenched, refused to discuss McCarthy and 'nearly speechless with emotion strode from the room. His eyes appeared moist.'

Eisenhower's position was weakened by his Vice-President, none other than Richard M. Nixon, at 39 the youngest ever in that office, and a champion of McCarthy. Nevertheless, by the beginning of 1954 it was obvious that McCarthyism was morally corrupting. It also appeared that there was evidence that McCarthy's right-hand man, Roy Cohn, was using his influence to obtain an Army Commission for one of his protegés. McCarthy was charged with using his position to blackmail army officers. After a gruelling Senate subcommittee enquiry, McCarthy was discredited and the unsavoury era of McCarthyism was over. It's effects lingered on: Charlie Chaplin, branded a Communist, never returned to America, and a question remained as to the guilt of the Rosenbergs, executed for spying at the height of anti-communist hysteria. Such was the public interest that the hearings were televised, attracting an audience of over twenty million viewers, who had already seen McCarthyism attacked on the small screen in Ed Murrows's CBS *See it Now* programmes, including 'The Case against Milo Radulovitch'.

It was not until the mid sixties that television eventually usurped newspapers as the prime opinion former but despite the inhibiting influence of commercial sponsors it was already becoming a major force, to such a degree that the fifties might be described as the Age of Television.

Left *Eisenhower survived McCarthy – and in 1956 was again 'marketed' in an electoral campaign which took the hard selling of politics even further.*

Above *Despite the bathos, Chaplin brought a strong element of social conscience to the early days of cinema. Although he was officially forgiven for his alleged Communist sympathies, he refused to return to America.*

With unintended irony, Post's feature article on a defecting Russian jet pilot shared the front cover with the ultimate image of consumerism – the car.

The Saturday Evening POST

October 9, 1954 – *15¢*

I FLEW MY MIG TO FREEDOM

By the Red Jet Pilot Who Won Our $100,000 Reward

NO PASSING

Right The television set emerged as the symbol of leisure and entertainment, as in this 1954 Pepsi ad.

AUDREY HEPBURN · FRED ASTAIRE

presented in a real new dimension in motion picture enjoyment!

Audrey's marvelous in her first musical ..singing and dancing with Fred to those great Gershwin tunes ...in the picture that presents the Paris fashions of tomorrow!

" 'FUNNY FACE' is truly an inspired picture... I would be very proud to have had 'Funny Face' to my credit." —Samuel Goldwyn

IN FUNNY FACE

co-starring KAY THOMPSON · with MICHEL AUCLAIR · ROBERT FLEMYNG

Music and Lyrics by GEORGE and IRA GERSHWIN · Choreography by Eugene Loring and Fred Astaire · Songs staged by Stanley Donen
Produced by Roger Edens · Directed by Stanley Donen · Written by Leonard Gershe · A Paramount Picture · TECHNICOLOR®

VistaVision®

8

CHAPTER TWO

THE AGE OF TELEVISION

MOTOROLA INTRODUCES AMERICA'S FINEST PORTABLE

The handle is to tune with!

Right in the handle–right up front–are pushbutton on-off, volume, station selector and fine tuning controls!

Feel like reaching out to touch the tuning handle on this new Motorola® Portable TV set?

Please do. Notice how you can watch the screen while you tune the set. The controls you use most are right in front where you want them.

Here, at last, is Portable TV that gives you console convenience and console performance, too. In fact, you almost forget this is a portable. You get big screen, big sound, big convenience *and* beauty. Plus many other features for more enjoyment.

Why not see the "Americana" at your Motorola Dealer now?

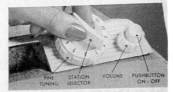

FINE TUNING   STATION SELECTOR   VOLUME   PUSHBUTTON ON - OFF

NEW MOTOROLA "AMERICANA"—Only Motorola gives you all this: exclusive tuning handle, Magic Mast antenna system, completely finished back, Zero-In Tuner, aluminum cabinet, earphone for private listening. Four 2-tone colors, super-power chassis, aluminized picture tube with 1-year warranty. Shown: 14P11-2, 14" over-all diagonal picture tube (104 sq. in. viewing area).

...and a new exclusive super-sensitive antenna!

Motorola's monopole MAGIC MAST antenna system out-performs rabbit-ear antennas . . . and telescopes into the cabinet.

⋀ MOTOROLA TV

World's Largest Exclusive Electronics Manufacturer   Specifications subject to change without notice. UHF opti.

By the late forties, it was obvious that television had arrived. Manufacturers who had been producing electronic items during the war went into making television sets. The public were fascinated with this fulfilment of their wartime expectations of a sci-fi future, and advertisers comparing their sales in those areas where television existed with those where they had to rely on the traditional media of newspapers and radio found that television advertising was producing dramatically increased sales. A lipstick manufacturer with an annual turnover of $50,000 began television advertising in 1950; as a direct result, within two years sales were up to $4,500,000.

The advertising factor ensured that television would be economically viable, something that had been an anxiety in the pioneering pre-war days. A further factor was the destruction of the traditional Hollywood film industry by the 1948 Supreme Court ruling (United States v Paramount *et al*) that the studios could no longer control cinemas, which had until then assured them audiences for their films and had excluded much of the work of foreign and small, independent studios. With the knowledge that only a small proportion of their output would find audiences under a system of free competition, productions were cut back almost overnight, throwing actors, technicians and writers into the job market.

Above *The new portable TV sets, such as this 1956 one, were compact but heavy. Nevertheless, they provided increased opportunities for constant television viewing.*

Left *Audrey Hepburn in* Funny Face *(1957) represented the new influence of Europe which was beginning to erode the superior insularity which had characterized America through the fifties.*

PHILCO

PHILCO *Predicta* TELEVISION

Not only could television draw on talents which might otherwise have found careers in films such as Lucille Ball and Desi Ainaz, whose *I Love Lucy* show was filmed in a small Hollywood studio (by 1955 the couple's company, Desilu, had bought up the old RKO studios), but it also attracted young theatre-trained actors, including Paul Newman, Rod Steiger, Sidney Poitier and Joanne Woodward. Together with young directors such as Arthur Penn and Sidney Lumet, these talents were drawn to the serious television drama found in such programmes as *Philco Television Playhouse, Goodyear Television* and *Kraft Television Theatre.* Not only was the drama of high quality, but the primitive production techniques of television at that time, with limited camera movement and no editing (television went out live) were more akin to theatre than cinema. These restrictions gave television an immediacy particularly in the use of close-ups which prompted Rod Steiger, who had starred in the successful *Goodyear Television Playhouse* production *Marty* to comment on "the immense power of that medium". Although this power was equally recognised by the advertisers, the limitations which made for good drama created many problems when commercials went out live: the true stories of the refrigerator door which refused to close and the dog which walked away from its supposedly irresistible food are now part of television history.

Above *The 1958 Philco Predicta separated screen and controls, and prior to the slimline tube represented the most successful attempt to reduce the bulk of TV sets.*

Right *The links between TV and advertising were not limited to the screen. Endorsement of products by stars, such as this 1953 cigarette advertisement featuring Lucille Ball, filled the popular magazines.*

Be WISE About KING SIZE

**Ask yourself...
Do you have *all* this with
your *present* cigarette?**

- Clean, fresh taste after smoking
- Full enjoyment of food
- Freedom from cigarette cough
- Mouth and throat comfort
- All day smoking enjoyment

See
LUCILLE BALL & DESI ARNAZ
starring in
"I LOVE LUCY" CBS-TV

If you answer "NO" to ANY of these questions—

IT'S TIME TO CHANGE TO PHILIP MORRIS!

Thousands are switching to PHILIP MORRIS King Size! Because this King
gives them every *good* thing they want in a cigarette.
That's why ... it's time for you to change to PHILIP MORRIS. Your *taste* can tell ...
your *throat* can tell that PHILIP MORRIS, King Size
or Regular, is America's *finest* cigarette.

REGULAR

CALL FOR PHILIP MORRIS

With ORLON these Fall Clothes are at Home in Soap and Water!

Today you want to spend more time with your children—and less time on clothes care. And now you can—thanks to Du Pont "Orlon". For here's a fiber that helps smart clothes take care of themselves. Take these twin sweaters, for instance. "Orlon" helps make them bright as rainbows...soft as a child's cheek...and a *delight* to wash. No stretching or blocking needed! Or take saucy pleated skirts like these. See how much better they act with "Orlon", too—stay pleat-perfect day after day. Dirty? Into the tub they go—come out looking new, with no more than a glance of an iron needed. So treat yourself—and all the family— to the fun of clothes of "Orlon" acrylic fiber. From fleece coats to fine lingerie, they're tailored to your easy-going yet on-the-go life today.

"Orlon" is Du Pont's trade-mark for its acrylic fiber

E. I. du Pont de Nemours & Co. (Inc.), Textile Fibers Department, Wilmington 98, Delaware

Du Pont makes fibers, does not make fabrics or merchandise

DU PONT
BETTER THINGS FOR BETTER LIVING
..THROUGH CHEMISTRY

ORLON® *one of Du Pont's modern-living fibers*
ACRYLIC FIBER

Even so, the power of television was sufficient for the new phenomenon of political advertising. Although the 1948 presidential campaign had been covered on television, broadcasting had proven a disaster for Dewey, who insisted on using the radio and television as a pulpit, and lost to Truman who instead had personally covered the country with rumbustious, barn-storming appearances. For the 1952 elections each move of Eisenhower's campaign was masterminded by an advertising agency. Not only were his appearances stage-managed for maximum impact so that they looked as good on television as they were effective live, but $1,500,000 worth of twenty-second advertising spots hit the screens in the last two weeks of the campaign. All heralded by the announcement 'Eisenhower answers the nation', they purported to deal with voters' questions. His opponent, Adlai Stevenson, refused to reduce politics to this level – to be marketed, as he put it, 'like a breakfast cereal'. In all probability, Eisenhower, the Old Soldier, needed all the guidance he could get to steer him into the White House. His Vice-President, Richard Nixon, was a different case. Nixon had learned how actors like Rod Steiger could appear to speak directly to the television viewer, and used this to great effect in the notorious 'Checkers' broadcast made during the campaign. It is even possible that it was this single appearance which won the election, so great was its impact.

Above *Ike and Mamie watch their protegé, Vice-President Nixon, make broadcasting history with his homely 'Checkers' speech. The nation swallowed the schmaltz, reached for its Kleenex and a political crisis was averted.*

Left *By 1953 the TV set had become almost mandatory as a graphic motif.*

Left *The ambitious young lawyer, Richard Nixon, had allied himself to the McCarthy camp which, while it lasted, was the most powerful clique in American politics.*

Above *The 'American Way of Life' took on a special, emotive significance and was to be defended against subversives who threatened it from within.*

Rumours had been building up that there had been misappropriation of campaign funds by Nixon, and there was pressure for him to withdraw from the campaign. Eisenhower was particularly concerned that there should be no taint of impropriety. Instead it was decided that Nixon would make a half hour television and radio broadcast to clear his name. So great was the public's interest that advertisers were vying with each other to sponsor the event, but rather than debase the occasion the Republicans financed it themselves.

Nixon's motto was to be 'sincerity is the quality that comes through on television', and 'Checkers', which he prepared himself was a masterpiece that had the nation dabbing its eyes at the thought that he should have been so wronged. With Mrs Nixon sitting by him, he spoke to the nation: 'Pat and I have the satisfaction that every dime that we've got is honestly ours. I should say this – that Pat doesn't have a mink coat, but she does have a respectable Republican cloth coat ... ' The clincher was the finale, the Checkers confession, describing how a man in Texas had heard that the Nixon's little girls wanted a dog, and how 'the day before we left on this campaign trip we got a message from Union Station in Baltimore saying they had a package for us. We went down to get it. You know what it was? It was a little cocker spaniel dog in a crate that he sent all the way from Texas. Black and white spotted. And our little girl – Tricia, the six-year-old – named it Checkers. And you know the kids love that dog and I just want to say this right now, that regardless of what they say about it, we're going to keep it!' With the parting shot, 'and remember, folks, Eisenhower is a great man, believe me. He is a great man ...', Nixon invited his audience to phone in with their judgement as to whether or not he should resign. Not only did the Checkers speech make political history, its innovation of the phone-in vote also anticipated elements of the television game show.

The biggest television event of the decade, however, was to come from England, with the coronation of Queen Elizabeth in 1952. It was American television treatment of this spectacular event that not only created something of a minor international incident (questions were asked about it in Parliament) but also seemed to symbolize the love-hate relationship between Britain and the phenomenon of 'Americanism' (in fashion, social behaviour, even politics) that was a constant theme of the decade. By now, television was quite well established in Britain, which had pioneered regular television broadcasting in 1936. After the war the production of television sets had resumed in 1946, and in 1949 the BBC acquired the Rank film studios and began work on a new television centre at White City. The next year Britain made its first international television broadcast to France. Even so, in 1951 only six per cent of Britain owned television sets, though the Coronation brought a rush of purchases and rentals.

Until 1955 the BBC had a monopoly in Britain of television broadcasting, and it was entirely independent of commercial sponsorship or advertising, although the possiblility of a second, commercial channel was under discussion. And not only was the BBC non-commercial, it was seen as an embodiment of pro-establishment values.

Right *The coronation inspired a craze for fashions influenced by its splendour. Cream and gold were prominent colours, and costume jewellery tiaras for evening wear made a brief appearance in America.*

Below *The coronation brought glamour to Britain in a spectacle which enthralled television viewers across the world, inspiring fashion designers and advertisers alike.*

To bring the Coronation to American viewers NBC-TV, in rivalry with CBS who had to date been the leaders in reportage, devised an ingenious system. With a specially equipped plane standing by, NBC filmed the BBC coverage straight off a television set. On the plane, the film was developed in specially-made tanks, and the film had been developed and edited by the time the plane arrived at Boston, where it was put out on the NBC network ahead of CBS (though later than ABC-TV, who had taken a cable link from the BBC's broadcast to Canada). Naturally the Coronation, attracting peak audiences, was targeted by advertisers, and it was the blatant use of tie-ins which so offended the British, whose approach to the event had been almost obsequious. Automobile manufacturers couldn't resist the puns of 'royal carriage' and 'Queen of the road', and, to the mortification of the British, a sequence of the Queen stepping from the Coronation coach appeared to metamorphose into Miss Pontiac of 1953 stepping from her car – 'body by Fisher'.

In Britain the anti-commercial television faction cited these examples as evidence of the lowering of standards which would occur if advertising were allowed. Nevertheless, at the end of 1953 the Government announced that it would allow a commercial television channel, which would be restricted to no more than six minutes of advertising per hour and which could not have sponsored programmes. To many, this was a further manifestation of the Americanisation of Britain, other examples including supermarkets, milk bars, teenagers, violent crime and popular music.

Above and **Right** *American companies saw the coronation, with its massive television and press coverage, as the perfect vehicle for advertising tie-ins, notwithstanding the inevitable incongruity of the images which resulted.*

Left *The theme of the 1958 Brussels Expo was the peaceful uses of atomic power.*

DOLLAR IMPERIALISM AND CULTURAL COLONISATION

Although American influence in Britain dates back to the twenties, culturally through films and music and economically through the taking over of British companies, it was the war which brought Britons into close contact with Americans, and the post-war economy which cemented America's economic influence. Unlike American civilians, whose standard of living had generally risen during the war and who had been encouraged to look forward to even greater peacetime prosperity as well as the benefits of wartime industrial development in an imagined future derived from science fiction, the expectations of the British were generally low, particularly as the evidence of the need to rebuild war-devastated cities was all around them.

At the end of 1946 the Britain Can Make It exhibition of post-war consumer products at the Victoria and Albert Museum attracted some million and a half visitors. Few of the products on show were available for domestic consumption, for the urgent need for export earnings took priority. Unfortunately, although buyers from 67 countries visited the exhibition, there was little to attract overseas markets. In any event, all hopes of peacetime prosperity were dashed in 1947 with the introduction of austerity measures, some of which were even harsher than the wartime deprivation.

The editor of *News Chronicle* suggested that rather than a design exhibition, a combination of design and industrial products together with a good dash of entertainment would make for a more useful exhibition and unlike the rushed-together Britain Can Make It, an event to mark the centenary of the 1851 Great Exhibition would allow for sufficient planning.

Below *Although dwarfed by domestic products, European imports such as the 'bubble car' and Morris Minor were amongst those which began to threaten the American car industry in the late fifties.*

Left *The 300-foot Skylon was the centrepiece of the 1951 Festival of Britain exhibition, though a cruel contemporary joke was that, slender and with no visible means of support, it also symbolized the British economy.*

Above *The Dome of Discovery exemplified the educational aspirations of the Festival.*

Right *The gothic town, built around the old shot tower, featured an artificial lake and fountains.*

The 1951 Festival of Britain – 'A Tonic to the Nation' – did little to promote consumer products, for the vetting carried out by the Council of Industrial Design allowed only for those products which complied with the current British design aesthetics. The director of the COID, justifying this policy, explained that 'our customers abroad are often more conscious of design than we are. How can we expect to produce a high standard for export unless we have a high standard at home?'

For the public design as a creed was no substitute for the consumables they craved. The director of the Festival struck the right note when he described it as 'fun, fantasy and colour'. In many ways, the festival was similar to the Coronation, both events producing a brief resurgence of national pride and an escape from austerity.

A more constant form of escapism could be found in American popular culture in the form of films and music. As in the past, cinema audiences could not help but enviously compare their lot with the American lifestyle, only now Britons were losing their passive acceptance that Hollywood was portraying an unobtainable dream world which was as remote as another planet. Magazines also brought the American lifestyle to Britain, and in the vicinity of American airbases the latest Detroit products, dwarfing the mainly pre-war British cars whose drivers were neurotically eking out their meagre petrol rations, swept past with insouciance.

The fascination with things American was not restricted to envious would-be consumers. The Independent Group of artists, architects and writers who were rejecting Britain's contemporary art scene looked to American Pop for its unpretentious vitality.

Looking back to that time, one of the Independent Group, the art critic Lawrence Alloway, wrote: 'we felt none of the dislike of commercial cultural standards amongst most intellectuals, but accepted it as a fact, discussed it in detail and consumed it enthusiastically. One result of our discussion was to take Pop culture out of the realm of 'escapism', 'sheer entertainment', 'relaxation' and to treat it with the seriousness of art. These interests put us in opposition both to the supporters of indigenous folk art and to the anti-American opinion in Britain.' The reference to 'folk art' derives from the craft tradition which characterized much British design – more related to the philosophy of William Morris than contemporary needs.

Bonanza (**below**) and Gunsmoke (**right**) became top rating television 'horse operas' and were extensively exported.

The climate of anti-Americanism was largely political. The Labour Government which came to power in the first post-war election in 1945, whilst backing America on Korea, was generally hostile both to American foreign policy and its domestic social values, as well as resentful for having been obliged to accept American foreign aid. This attitude was reflected in such official bodies as the Council of Industrial Design, and anti-Americanism became a manifestation of moral and aesthetic puritanism. British rejection of austerity was proclaimed in the return of Winston Churchill in the 1951 election, an immediate effect of which was a return to friendly Anglo-American relations, with an agreement over the continued use of Britain for USAF defence bases, and the emergence of Britain as an atomic power.

The British atom bomb was tested in 1952. Although its development had been carried out under the Labour Government, it had kept its existence secret as the official Labour policy was against atomic weapons. Now the era of austerity seemed to be coming to a close. Both rationing and the 'utility' scheme (under which furniture and other items had been manufactured in accordance with official standards to ensure a good basic quality of fabrication and design during the war and post-war period) were ended, and in theory the way was open for Britain to become a consumer society. Only two things stood in the way – the lack of domestically produced consumer goods and restrictions still limiting imports.

The Conquest of Everest in 1953 by Edmund Hillary and his Sherpa companion, Tenzing Norkay, was also a triumph of technology in the expedition's use of nylon clothing and lightweight oxygen equipment.

Left *Tenzing plants the Nepalese flag on the 29,002-foot summit of Everest. The Union Jack and United Nations flag were also planted.*

Above *Edmund Hillary and Tenzing after their triumph.*

ON TOP OF THE WORLD Tenzing braces self against wind which sends flags of U.N., Great Britain and Nepal fluttering wildly on ice ax handle. Rope over his left foot runs to Hillary, who took picture.

At about the same time, America was embarking on a policy of domestic growth which would characterise the Eisenhower years as the biggest ever consumer bonanza. American domestic consumer production found itself threatened by the European industries America had helped in the post-war period.

Whilst the seventeen billion dollar 'imperialism' of the Marshall Plan was motivated more by the need to achieve European stability and counter the influence of communism, there were other programmes of assistance. The Committee for Assistance and Distribution of Materials to Artisans, and Handicraft Development Incorporated sponsored Italian design, which had been repressed under Fascism. Leading American industrial designers arranged for such basic tools as drawing aids and instruments to be sent to Italy. In 1947 the charitable Handicraft Development Inc. opened an outlet for Italian products, The House of Italian Handicrafts in New York, and began a programme of market research to discover what Italian products would succeed in the American market.

Olivetti's Lexicon 80 *(***below***) and the Robbiati domestic Expresso maker (***right***) demonstrated that, despite having been considered by Americans as mainly craft-orientated, Italy was poised to be a major contributor to industrial design.*

The motor scooter became a symbol of Italy's post-war industrial regeneration, as well as continental chic.

Italian imports were subsidized by four and a half million dollars of credit via the Export-Import Bank. Although the assistance of Marshall aid was to put Italian industry back on its feet and introduce American mass-production techniques, no-one foresaw the incredible rate at which it would expand. Neither of the major post-war Italian exhibitions, the 1946 RIMA exhibition of home furnishings and the 1947 Triennale, gave the American Industrial designers any indication that their pre-eminence would eventually be challenged. In 1949 the Art Institute of Chicago planned an exhibition of Italian craft and design which would tour America. A group from the project, headed by the designer Walter Dorwin

Teague, toured Italy selecting over two thousand items for the exhibition. Although most were craft products, they also included Gio Ponti's espresso coffee machine designed for La Pavoni in 1949, the Olivetti Lexicon 80 typewriter, designed by Marcello Nizzoli in 1948, and Corradino D'Ascanio's 1946 Vespa motor scooter. Nevertheless, the exhibition Italy at Work emphasized the non-industrial side of design. Teague commented that during his visit he had found Italian designers 'frolicking like boys let out of school', and in his introduction to the exhibition catalogue wrote that its purpose was to stimulate 'the importation of Italian craft works into America, and so assist the craftsmen and improve the dollar position without competing with American industry'. He went on to place Italians firmly in the Craft Camp: 'I'm no traitor to mass production, which enables Americans as a whole to enjoy far better-designed products and many more of them than are available to the mass of Italians, but a designer could not help but be delighted and stimulated by the daring *tours de force* his Italian colleagues could indulge in at will.'

The carefree Italian image, as portrayed in the 1953 Gregory Peck and Audrey Hepburn film *Roman Holiday*, influenced American automobile design towards a lightness which, with the exception of Raymond Loewy's Euro-influenced designs for Studebaker, was generally lacking. It was the Italian and British sports cars whose popularity as imports was responsible for the 1953 Chevrolet Corvette, the first American sports car, and the 1954 Ford Thunderbird, neither of which had any precedent in American automobile styling.

Raymond Loewy's Studebaker avoided the excesses which characterized American car design, incorporating instead European sleekness, lightness and elegance.

A similar exercise was undertaken with German industrial design, culminating in the 1949 exhibition at the Museum of Science and Industry in New York of products from over three hundred manufacturers from within the American-controlled zone of occupation. So as not to offend American sensibilities it was stressed that the exhibition, approved by the Economic Co-operation Administration, the State Department and the Army, was free of any items tainted by Nazism. Although the majority of exhibits were of a craft or light industrial nature, there was also a Volkswagen which was of course very much a Nazi item, having been expressly designed by Dr Porsche as the 'People's car' as part of Nazi ideology. A contemporary article noted that it was inconceivable that German products would ever compete with American mass-production. Nevertheless, by 1958 European small car imports, headed by the Volkswagen, were threatening the American automobile which embodied the excesses of the fifties creed of Planned Obsolescence and Conspicuous Consumption.

Further evidence of American interest in foreign design was the opening of Swedish Modern Inc. New York in 1950 and the Japan Trade Centre in New York in 1954. Although it can thus be seen that America was by no means isolationist on design matters, it nevertheless had a paternalistic attitude to foreign design, based on its postion as the world's most powerful industrial nation. Not only had America virtually invented the concepts of industrial design, packaging and marketing, all based on the foundation of mass production (which had been pioneered by Henry Ford), but from the late forties and through the fifties it gave the world its architecture in the form of International Modernism and major contributions to fine art. By the mid fifties a new phenomenon appeared to symbolize America to the rest of the world: rock 'n' roll.

Left *Grundig were among several German manufacturers whose products, such as this 1957 radiogram, found a growing acceptance of European consumer products in the USA.*

Right *The rapid growth in transatlantic air travel did much to expose America to European influences.*

FIRST JETS ON THE ATLANTIC...FIRST ON THE PACIFIC...FIRST IN LATIN AMERICA...FIRST 'ROUND THE WORLD

6½ MAGIC HOURS TO EUROPE

The first Jet Clippers that you will ride in are Boeing 707s, the most thoroughly flight-tested aircraft ever to enter commercial service.

Join the first Jet travelers across the Atlantic

Starting this Fall: The No. 1 airline across the Atlantic welcomes you to a magic world of travel! Fares as low as $453⁶⁰ round trip to London, $489⁶⁰ to Paris . . . daily from New York.

Pan Am's Jet Clippers* are the first transatlantic jet airliners. They are *pure* jets, a major advance over turbo-props. Four massive jet engines give you beautifully quiet, vibration-free comfort at 600 mph.

Jet Clippers will offer the finest, fastest transatlantic service. No increase in minimum fares. Coming: Jets to Latin America, the Pacific and 'round the world.

For Fall reservations to Europe on the new Jet Clippers, call your Travel Agent or one of the 53 offices of Pan Am in the U. S. and Canada. For a free, colorful, fact-filled Jet brochure, write: Pan American, Dept. 707, Box 1790, New York 17, N.Y. *Trade-Mark, Reg. U.S. Pat. Off.

PAN AM

Pan American, world's most experienced airline, carries almost as many people to Europe as the next 2 airlines combined

45

CHAPTER FOUR

ROLL OVER, BEETHOVEN

Since the twenties America had been seen as the land of fads and crazes, some which were simply that, and others which were manifestations of social changes which would eventually appear in other countries. Some of these changes would have happened anyway, for the same reasons that they had in America, but even so the influence of America was blamed for various post-war social phenomena, such as the rise in divorce, juvenile delinquency and the growth of leisure time.

During the fifties there was a plethora of fads and crazes, ranging from Davy Crockett (who, now immortalised by Disney became a marketing goldmine. Coonskin caps, lunch boxes, pup tents and toys, four million records of the Ballad of Davy Crockett and fourteen million Davy Crockett books totalled some hundred million dollars worth of sales during seven months of Crockett madness) to Hula Hoops and 3D movies. To the outside world there was little to distinguish these from action painting, instant coffee, flying saucers and everything else American.

Even America treated the teenage explosion as a passing phase. It first became apparent during the war, when it was explained as the result of abnormal social conditions, and thereafter was the subject of analysis by teachers and church leaders, parents and sociologists, all of whom, whilst varying in their attitudes, were in agreement that it would not last. During the forties and the early fifties scant attention was paid to teenagers as consumers, and even that music which had strong youth appeal was not directed at them. So that for example neither Frank Sinatra nor Johnnie Ray could now be regarded as teen-orientated. With the advent of rock 'n' roll the young became consumers to be specifically targeted.

Right *Davy Crockett had been an insignificant Walt Disney children's television show until the craze suddenly took off. While it lasted virtually anything with a Crockett image would sell, although its equally sudden demise prompted one manufacturer to rue that 'kids were as fickle as women'.*

Left *1958 saw the Hula Hoop craze, which spread from the USA (where some thirty million were sold) to the rest of the world — Moscow condemned it as exemplifying 'the emptiness of American Culture'.*

The roots of the music are varied and include black church spirituals and gospel, R&B, Country (rockabilly and Western swing), Jump and Cajun. Because of this, rock 'n' roll can be seen as the synthesis of American folk music. Socially, its greatest significance was the fusion of black and white music, which was itself both the reason for much of the opposition that rock 'n' roll encountered and a contributory factor to the erosion of racialism.

Until rock 'n' roll, black music had been specifically marketed as such. Major record companies had separate 'race music' catalogues and race music had its own hit charts. Since the late forties there had been a number of small black-only recording companies who would licence hit material to the major producers. Radio stations were often segregated, some being black-only. Apart from national hits, music was still quite regional, and as rock 'n' roll developed in different areas these regional variations appeared in the music.

Right *By 1958 jiving had become sufficiently acceptable to be featured in this floorwax ad.*

Opposite *Alan Freed claimed to have invented the term* rock 'n' roll, *which he even tried to copyright. Here in 1955 at the New York radio station WINS, Freed fans sport rock 'n' roll jackets.*

The popularizing of rock 'n' roll is usually attributed to the white disc jockey Alan Freed who claimed to have invented the term, and even tried to copyright it and earn a royalty every time it appeared in a song or film. It was actually by no means new, having been a black slang euphemism for sex, but as it was not a term white audiences would generally know Freed used it to mask the black origins of the R&B he was putting over to his audience of white college kids on Cleveland's WJW radio (a 'good music' station that would not have countenanced obvious 'race music'). Even so it soon became obvious that Freed's 'Moondogs' Rock 'n' Roll Party' show was really playing black R&B and when, shortly after introducing rock 'n' roll in 1952, he sponsored a Moondog Ball in Cleveland the event had to be cancelled — not only because some twenty five thousand people turned up at a hall with a capacity for half that number, but more significantly because despite the city's segregationist policies the crowd was equally made up of blacks and whites. Freed's DJ technique was unique — the party atmosphere generated by manic comments and the music often accompanied by his beating time with a telephone directory smashed down on the table.

CLOTHES: ABERCROMBIE AND FITCH

Almost everyone appreciates the best

DRINK
Coca-Cola
TRADE-MARK ®
ICE COLD

The first nationally known rock 'n' roll band was Bill Haley and his Comets. Originally an unassuming little Western Swing Combo (the Saddlemen), Haley had recorded a cover of Jackie Brenston's 'Rocket 88' in 1951, and by 1952 the renamed Comets were making R&B 'jump' style rockers like 'Rock the Joint'. 'Rock Around the Clock' first appeared in 1954, achieving only minor hit status. The next year it was used in the 'teenage delinquent' movie, *The Blackboard Jungle*. The notoriety of the film and its controversial subject not only popularized the music but also cemented the public prejudice that rock 'n' roll was synonymous with juvenile delinquency.

Compared with black R&B, the Comets were pretty tame, and even though they acquired an avid following Haley himself was not superstar material. Rock 'n' roll had not yet produced a cult figure equal to, for example, Marlon Brando or James Dean, or even Frank Sinatra or Johnnie Ray. Such a figure was about to emerge, however, in the person of Elvis Presley.

LET'S HAVE A PAJAMA PARTY!

Top left *In 1954, with the rock 'n' roll revolution about to burst onto the scene, teenagers still had a socially clean-cut image.*

Below left *Coca-Cola had been featuring teenagers in their campaigns since the forties. In this 1953 ad the wholesome image still prevails.*

By 1957 Elvis was considered sufficiently acceptable to be allowed to appear in a teenage girl's bedroom in this advertisement for Canada Dry.

In 1956 Elvis was the raw energy of rock 'n' roll personified. He can be credited with fusing together strands of different musical influences (and early nicknames such as the 'Hillbilly Cat' and 'The King of Western Bop' show how hard it was to label him before rock 'n' roll became an identifiable sound) to which he added his unique ingredient of charismatic sexuality.

The regional nature of minority music gave Presley, in common with many other early white rock 'n' rollers, a varied mixture of influences. From his early childhood in Mississippi he absorbed the local black blues sound, exemplified by the singers Big Bill Broonzy and Arthur Crudup, as well as country and western and gospel. At the age of thirteen his musical environment changed when his family moved to Memphis, the centre of Southern black music. Sam Phillips, destined to make history by first recording Presley, ran

the Memphis Recording Service 'for Negro artists in the South who wanted to make a record [but] just had no place to go', where he recorded the likes of Howlin' Wolf, Bobby 'Blue' Bland, Little Junior Parker and B.B. King. Although the popular perception of the South is of a segregationalist society, poor whites co-existed with the blacks, many young whites not only absorbing the music but styles of dress and speech. According to legend, Sam Phillips, who initially leased his recordings to major labels rather than market

them himself, had worked out that a winning formula would be a white singer who sounded black. 'If I could find a white man who had the Negro sound and the Negro feel I could make a billion dollars,' he is reported to have said. Although accounts vary as to the exact circumstances in 1954 Presley's recordings of 'That's all Right' (an Arthur Crudup song) and 'Blue Moon of Kentucky' were issued by Phillips's Sun Label (he had changed the name from Memphis Recording Service in 1952). Advanced promotional play on

In 1955, the year of this picture, teenagers jiving to rock 'n' roll were still enough of a novelty to be considered newsworthy.

the local radio resulted in it being a minor sensation; it was briefly number one in the Memphis Country and Western Charts and warranted Presley's number eight position in the national music paper *Billboard*'s annual review of promising hillbilly newcomers.

He became a local celebrity (although his appearance on the Grand Ole Oprey was a flop he became a regular on the Louisiana Hayride) and began touring with his band in Texas and Mississippi. The singer Bob Luman has left an account of a Presley performance of this time, which is quoted in Paul Hemphill's *Nashville Sound*: 'This cat came out in red pants and a green coat and a pink shirt and socks, and he had this sneer on his face and he stood behind the mike for five minutes, I'll bet, before he made a move. Then he hit his guitar a lick and he broke two strings. I'd been playing ten years and I hadn't broken a *total* of two strings. So there he was, these two strings dangling, and he hadn't done anything yet,

and these high school girls were screaming and fainting and running up to the stage, and then he started to move his hips real slow like he had a thing for his guitar . . .'

Two years later television viewers were to be astounded by Presley's act. Now managed by Tom Parker ('when I first knew Elvis he had a million dollars' worth of talent. Now he has a million dollars'), Presley had left Sun and was now recording for RCA. After two innocuous appearances on the *Dorsey Brothers' Show* on CBS in 1958 he treated NBC's *Milton Berle Show* to a full-blooded performance and attracted a storm of protest. Trotting out the routine cliché which linked rock 'n' roll with juvenile delinquency, Jack

Gould wrote in the *New York Times*: 'These gyrations have to concern parents unless we're the kind of parents who approve of kids going around stealing hubcaps, indulging in promiscuity and generally behaving like delinquents . . . it isn't enough to say that Elvis is kind to his parents, sends money home and is the same unspoilt kid he was before all the commotion began. That still isn't a free ticket to behave like a sex maniac in public before millions of impressionable kids.'

Below In 1956 Elvis had a wild stage act and hordes of female fans.
Right 1957 – as pop music and the youth image became a phenomenon to be reckoned with, advertisers began to capitalize on the image and the language.

NEARLY EVERYONE KNOWS BY NOW—

Pontiac's Got a Hit!

* Seems like everybody's got an eye for this fresh and frisky beauty! And why not? It's a '57 Pontiac, the top crowd pleaser of the year, with over *6 dozen* "firsts" to its credit. There's the all-new "going places" look of Star Flight body design. There's years-ahead riding smoothness with new cradle-soft Level-Line suspension. There are new controls that command instant wheel obedience, PLUS a brand-new V-8 engine superior even to last year's world-record Strato-Streak! And when you take all these big-time changes and improvements and polish them to perfection in a rugged *100,000-mile Marathon Run*, you've really got something. You've got, in fact, America's No. 1 Road Car. Come in and try it. You'll be a Pontiac fan for life!

AMERICA'S NUMBER ① ROAD CAR!

SEE YOUR PONTIAC DEALER

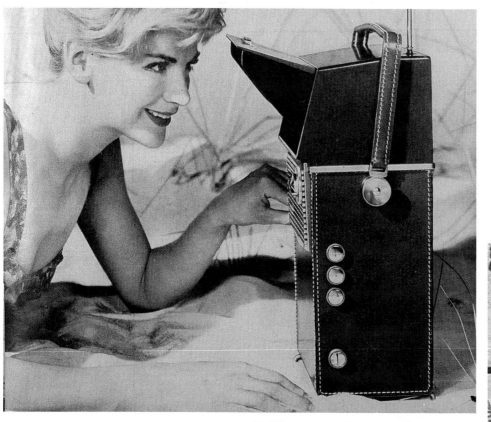

Left *The 1959 Philco Safari was the first battery-powered TV. Only 17 inches and weighing 15 lbs, it was advertised as bringing television to picnics, the beach, boats and trains. Costing about twice the amount of a conventional TV, however, it was an expensive novelty.*

Presley had pushed the *Berle Show*'s ratings up past Phil Silvers' *Sergeant Bilko* and, though insisting on the act being toned down, NBC were content to risk the critics' wrath for the sake of ratings, booking Presley to work the same magic for Steve Allen, Ed Sullivan's only rival for Sunday night prime time. Sullivan had been a vocal critic of Presley, describing him as 'unfit for family viewing'. That Presley was to notch up three million-selling hits during the year – 'Heartbreak Hotel', 'Don't be Cruel' and 'Love me Tender' – was of no interest to Sullivan, but ratings were another matter. When the figures were revealed (Presley's appearance had put Allen's share of that night's viewers up to 55.3% against Sullivans meagre 14.8%) he had no choice. Sullivan booked him for three shows for a staggering $50,000 (Steve Allen had paid $5,500), but took the precaution of ensuring that the cameras only showed from the waist up, thus avoiding any unpleasantness about pelvic gyrations. CBS got good value for their money, with the first show attracting 54 million viewers.

Below *Hi-fi units became high priced consumer items, creating a huge market for LPs. Relatively little pop music appeared on LPs, but the teenage singles market was seen as leading up to the purchase of expensive equipment in the future.*

Introducing

The *Smaller* **SONY** TR-610

6 TRANSISTOR SUPERHET

SIZE......4.2" x 2.5" x 1"   WEIGHT......9 OZS

COLOR...RED, BLACK, GREEN, IVORY WITH GOLD

SONY CORP.   TOKYO, JAPAN

CABLE ADDRESS — SONYCORP TOKYO

Nevertheless, many felt that Ed Sullivan had betrayed them. 'Presley and his voodoo of frustration and defiance have become symbols in our country, and we are sorry to come upon Ed Sullivan in the role of promoter' (*Catholic Sun*), and 'On the *Ed Sullivan Show* programme Presley injected movements of the tongue and indulged in wordless singing that were singularly distasteful. When Presley executes his bumps and grinds it must be remembered by Columbia Broadcasting System that even the twelve-year-old's curiosity may be overstimulated' (*New York Times*).

Above *The miniature portable radio, shown in this 1958 advertisement, became a standard accessory, although by present standards its sound was definitely tinny.*

The rock 'n' roll scene had been developing during Presley's rise to stardom. Alan Freed had moved on from Cleveland and since 1954 had been doing his radio show from New York (on a salary of $70,000 a year) as well as promoting Moondog Shows at the Brookland Paramount. Some three and a half thousand rock 'n' roll DJ's were at work, though many were under fire for promoting juvenile delinquency or moral delinquency or black music or anything the moral majority could think up. Much of the music was now overtly commercial, especially as record companies had come up with a solution to the racial issues posed by black performers by issuing white cover-versions. Freed stayed true to his roots by only playing original recordings, as did some of the others. Just across the border from Del Rio, Texas, the legendary Wolfman Jack howled at the moon and spread rock 'n' roll anarchy between playing the best of R&B and rockabilly. So powerful were the Wolfman's transmissions that some nights he could be heard in California and right up to Canada.

Whilst Freed and the Wolfman kept the faith, the major record companies, though happy to mine the rich seam of rock 'n' roll, still saw it as a passing phase, particularly as a relatively high proportion of hits were in the hands of small, independent companies. Hoping to get away from the controversies surrounding rock 'n' roll, the major companies tried to replace it with Calypso music and, through active promotion, created a small Calypso boom in 1957. In any event, in March 1958 the era came to an abrupt end when, for a bargain $82 a month as opposed to his normal $100,000, the US Army gained Presley for the next two years.

Above *The circle skirt, introduced in 1950, had a tendency to flare up when the wearer jived, and became a favoured dress for extrovert rock 'n' rollers.*

Right *Elvis had already been tamed by Parker, RCA and Hollywood; the US Army proved that an era was truly at an end.*

FASHION

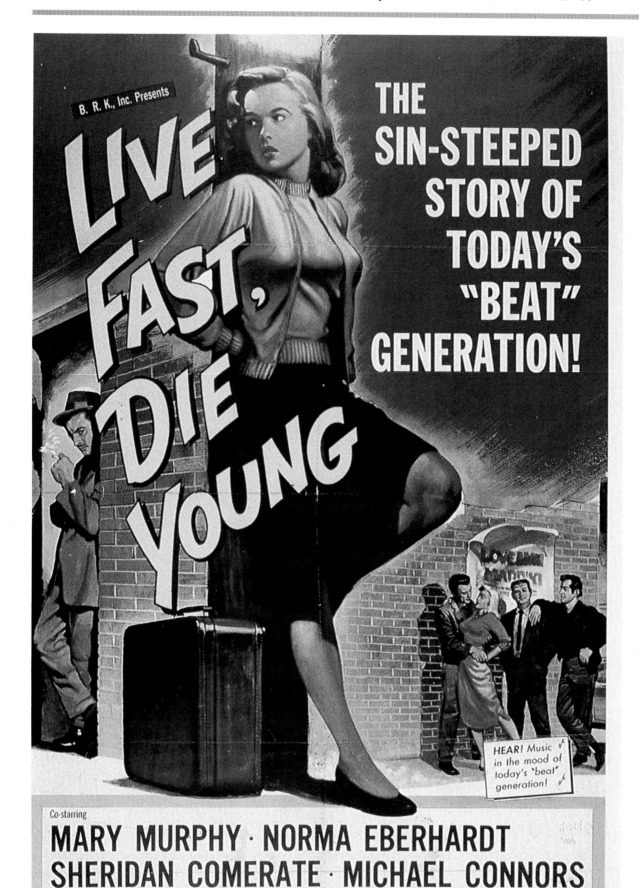

The sensationalist promise of an exposé of 'sin-steeped' youth and the music in the mood of 'today's beat generation' advertise this 1958 teen-exploitation B-movie.

CHAPTER FIVE

LIVE FAST, DIE YOUNG

With Presley safely in the army, many hoped that rock 'n' roll was finished, and with it the tumultuous years of teenage rebellion. Because it was such a popular subject in the B-movies of the fifties, the manifestation of juvenile delinquency is often dismissed as a period cult theme, rather like invaders from outer space or giant killer ants. The subject is also made ridiculous by its constant link with rock 'n' roll – which Frank Sinatra described as 'the martial music of every sideburned delinquent', while Judge Hilda Schwartz of the New York Adolescent Court pontificated: 'for the disturbed, hostile and insecure youth, the stimulation of this frenzied,

abandoned music certainly can't be therapy.'

Nevertheless, juvenile delinquency was a serious social problem, and one which statistics showed was getting worse in the course of the decade. For example, the summer of 1956 produced a 26% increase in possession of dangerous weapons. Teenagers became universally branded with the delinquent image. 'I'm Not a Juvenile Delinquent' sang Frankie Lymon and the Teenagers in the 1957 film *Rock Rock Rock*. Lymon was himself only fifteen years old, but a year later started the drug habit that killed him in 1968.

Juvenile delinquency existed before rock 'n' roll; it is manifest in Graham

Greene's *Brighton Rock*, for example, or, again in Britain, in the controversial Craig – Bentley case of 1951: Christopher Craig described by the Lord Chief Justice as 'one of the most dangerous criminals ever to stand in the dock' was only sixteen when he shot a policeman – his accomplice Derek Bentley, who had been armed with a knife and knuckleduster, was nineteen, which qualified him for hanging.

The 1955 song 'Black Denim Trousers and Motorcycle Boots' tells how the rider met his end on Route 101.

Even the movie that inspired countless later imitations in the B-movie teen-pic genre, Stanley Kramer's *The Wild One* of 1953, was based on a true event from the forties. In 1947 a band of maverick bikers turned up at Hollister, a small Californian town. Beer drinking led to minor vandalism which quickly degenerated into violence; many people were injured and the town hall was wrecked. Although extreme, this was only one of many such postwar incidents, so *The Wild One* was an examination of a pre-existent condition, not the instigator as was often subsequently alleged. What the film did, however, was give the phenomenon style. Through his presence, Marlon Brando endowed the character Johnny (leader of one of the gangs) with an introspective romantic quality, whilst those attracted to pure aggression could look to Lee Marvin (who became the cinema's archtypal 'baddie', disfiguring Gloria Grahame's face with scalding coffee in *The Big Heat*, 1953, and again portraying evil in *Bad Day at Black Rock*, 1955) who played the rival leader. Brando's Johnny voiced the nihilism that characterized the delinquent; asked 'What are you rebelling against?', he makes the classic retort 'What have you got?' Similarly, *Life* magazine's photo-journalistic report, following Harrison Salisbury's book *The Shook-up Generation*, pictured a youth leaning back against a jukebox: 'What do you like to read?' – 'Nothin'. I don't like to read.' – 'What do you like to do?' 'Sit.' – 'Just sit?' – 'Just sit.'

By the time Vertigo *was released in 1958 the European influence was being widely felt in the American cinema and advertising industry.*

Dragstrip Girl (1957) was yet another exploitation movie that followed in the wake of Rebel Without a Cause, complete with its own chicken run scene.

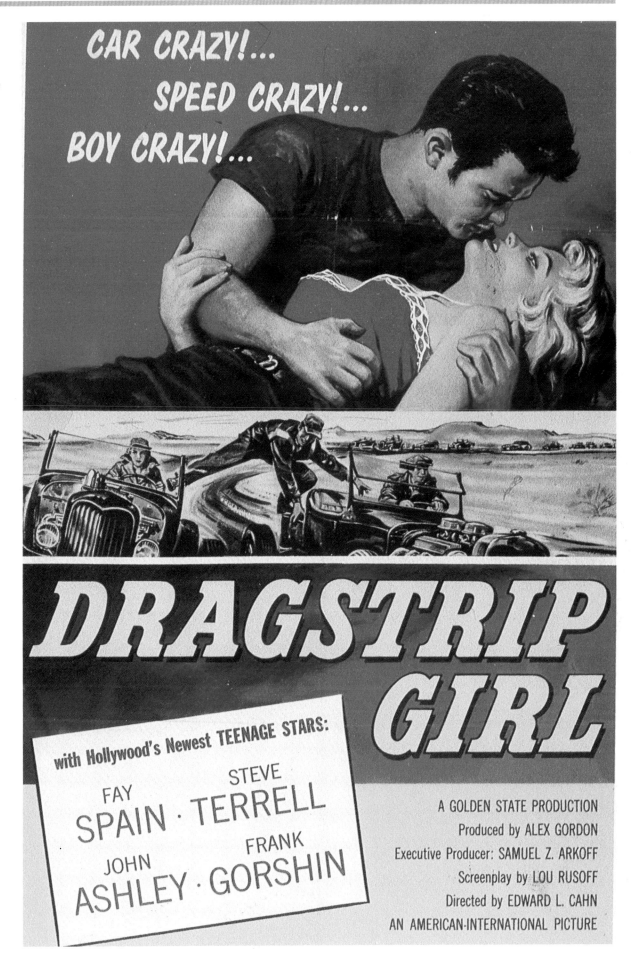

CAR CRAZY!...
SPEED CRAZY!...
BOY CRAZY!...

DRAGSTRIP GIRL

with Hollywood's Newest TEENAGE STARS:

FAY SPAIN · STEVE TERRELL
JOHN ASHLEY · FRANK GORSHIN

A GOLDEN STATE PRODUCTION
Produced by ALEX GORDON
Executive Producer: SAMUEL Z. ARKOFF
Screenplay by LOU RUSOFF
Directed by EDWARD L. CAHN
AN AMERICAN-INTERNATIONAL PICTURE

Fearful that it might be inspirational, many places in America banned *The Wild One* and Britain banned it completely, although the French watched it and French youths adopted biker style to become the 'Blousons Noirs'. *The Wild One* opened the way to a spate of teen films through the fifties. An early one was Universal's *Girls in the Night*, 1953, which was described as 'the first shocking story of teenage delinquent girls'. Many others followed, the most famous being Roger Corman's *Teenage Doll*, 1957, billed as 'the scorching truth about today's thrill-mad hellcats'.

The issue of teenage delinquency was by now a common topic for the press, sermons and PTA meetings.

Television, with its small screen violence, was frequently seen as a contributor to the problem. In 1954 Evan Hunter's novel *The Blackboard Jungle*, an examination of violence in a city high school, publicized the anti-authoritarianism teachers were experiencing in the classrooms. Appearing the next year as a film, it cemented the association between rock 'n' roll and delinquency by its use of Bill Haley's 1954 song 'Rock Around the Clock' in the soundtrack. The record was re-issued in the wake of the film and eventually became the best known rock 'n' roll song ever, with sales of some thirty million. Although *The Blackboard Jungle* was not claiming the problem was universal – it showed by way of

contrast another school which was problem free – the film did nothing to lessen it or hold out any hope of a solution instead; like *The Wild One*, it was accused of providing role models.

Below *Teenage sex was not confined to exploitation movies. Elia Kazan's film of Tennessee William's* Baby Doll *created a wave of controversy in 1956, bringing calls for more stringent censorship. Time magazine called it 'just possibly the dirtiest American picture ever legally exhibited', which, with similar condemnations, actually made it a box office hit and Baby Doll pyjamas became a fashion craze.*

Left *Ed Byrnes, who played the jive-talking car park attendant Kookie on TV in* 77 Sunset Strip *recorded 'Lend Me Your Comb' with Connie Stevens in 1959. Like the classic 'Blue Suede Shoes' it satirized teenage male narcissism.*

THE BITTER DISPUTE OVER 'BABY DOLL'

Although her memorable performance contributes to the success of the rock 'n' roll movie The Girl Can't Help It, *it is inconceivable that Jayne Mansfield (in the role taken by Natalie Wood) could have done anything but trivialize* Rebel Without a Cause.

Now juvenile problems had become a marketable film theme. When Warner Bros. were offered *Rebel Without a Cause* they saw it as a teen movie and an ideal film for their two new youth stars, Tab Hunter and Jayne Mansfield – striking evidence of the commercial exploitation of the teen market that characterized the era. Fortunately, at the insistence of the director Nicholas Ray, Warner accepted his choice of James Dean (who had just finished his first film, *East of Eden*) and Natalie Wood. Both Nicholas Ray and the writer Stewart Stern undertook lengthy research, attending juvenile courts and interviewing delinquents, police, probation officers and criminal psychiatrists. The presence of Dean in the character of Jim added raw power to the film's realism and the shock value of a story which put juvenile delinquency in the context of middle class affluence. Dean's death before the release of *Rebel* sparked off the 'live fast, die young' teenage creed, which was seen as a natural reaction to life lived under the threat of atomic war. James Dean's last film *Giant* was released the year after his death. By then he was already a legend, quickly exploited in the 1957 Robert Altman film *The James Dean Story*.

Right *The powerful 'chicken run' sequence in* Rebel Without a Cause *inspired similar scenes in many teen-exploitation movies such as* Dragstrip Girl *(1957).*

Juvenile Jungle of 1958 yet again exploited the formula of teenage sex and violence. The salacious imagery of the publicity poster was an almost standard presentation for this sort of film, which cynically fuelled the hysteria surrounding the juvenile delinquent phenomenon.

Nothing after *Rebel Without a Cause* managed to transcend straightforward commercial teen exploitation. The success of Haley's music in *The Blackboard Jungle* gave rise to a stream of rock 'n' roll movies whose story was of secondary importance. Haley's 'Rock Around the Clock' success was exploited in a film of the same name in 1956, closely followed by a sequel in the same year, *Don't Knock the Rock*, both overshadowed by the fifties rock 'n' roll movie classic, *The Girl Can't Help It*. In Elvis Presley's second film *Jailhouse Rock* (1957) rock 'n' roll was again linked to violent, anti-social behaviour, as it was in *High School Confidential* (1958) which was distinguished both by Jerry Lee Lewis's theme song and its juvenile drug abuse theme – which was also the subject of *The Cool and the Crazy* in the same year. 1958 also produced *Juvenile Jungle* and *Let's Rock*. In addition to countless other rock 'n' roll movies (virtually every major performer was featured on film and even Alan Freed, father of rock 'n' roll, was himself featured in *Mr Rock 'n' Roll* the teen delinquent theme film proliferated: *The Hot Rod Rumble* (1957) which double-billed with *Rock All Night*, *Dragstrip Girl* (1958), *Hot Rod Gang* (1958), *The Ghost of Dragstrip Hollow* (1959) and *Dragstrip Riot* (1959).

Away from the burning rubber, teen movies (most of which had great titles if little else) tended towards sensationalism, as promised in the publicity material. *Running Wild* (1955) was advertised as 'Stark, savage truth stabs from the Juke Box Jungle – the first jolting story of organised teenage gangs', and *Juvenile Jungle* (1958) offered 'A girl delinquent. . . . a jet propelled gang . . . out for fast kicks!' Robert Altman's *The Delinquents* (1957) was followed by *Untamed Youth* (1957), which starred Mamie Van Doren; the *Party Crashers* and *Live Fast, Die Young* in 1958; and *Lost, Lonely and Vicious* in 1959. Despite their lurid titles, these films generally portrayed a moralising attitude to the teenage phenomenon.

MURDER...
AT 120
MILES PER HOUR!!

DRAGSTRIP RIOT

starring

YVONNE LIME · GARY CLARKE · FAY WRAY · BOB TURNBULL · CONNIE STEVENS

Dragstrip Riot (1958) pushed home the message that teenagers were violent. Drag racing, which had first become popular as a legitimate and respectable sport, became tarnished by its association with illegal road racing and chicken runs.

Polecat, Redskin egghead; Appassionata Von Climax, a millionaire-beguiling Big City gal; Sydney the Parrot, a bird with Big Ideas; Pig Gal, a grubby menace; Stone Age Gal, a passionate giantess; The Three Teenagers; Moonbeam McSwine who fancies pigs; and Li'l Abner's Daisy Mae with Honest Abe.

teen-age kissin' cousin; Miss Mizzou from Missouri; Savannah Gay, actress; Summer Olson, sweet but married; Cheetah, the pert Oriental; Herself Muldoon, underworld queen; Gilberta Hall, blind and lovely; Doe Redwood, pilot; Feeta-Feeta, secretary; Deen Wilderness, doctor; and Madame Lynx, spy.

Above *Whilst America continued its love affair with the car, a few brave souls, such as this 1957 Jersey City student, braved ridicule and took to the Italian motor scooter. Although* Roman Holiday *had briefly popularized the scooter, it nevertheless had an unmanly image amongst the young until the following decade when British Mods gave it street credibility.*

Left *Although rock 'n' roll, television and teen movies produced a new generation of pop heroes, the funny pages continued to entertain with the bizarre cartoon characters of Al Capp and Milton Caniff.*

It really did seem that every aspect of the teenage phenomenon had been fully exploited as box-office fodder. All that was left was to combine it with another popular fifties cult genre, the monster movie, to produce gems like *Monster on the Campus* in 1959 (made by Jack Arnold, director of *High School Confidential*, who also had made such classics as *The Creature from the Black Lagoon* and the *Incredible Shrinking Man*), *I Was a Teenage Werewolf* and *I Was a Teenage Frankenstein* (1957).

To an extent, these teen/monster movies were a logical resolution of the whole vexed issue. After all the soul searching by concerned seniors, the questions posed by *The Wild One* and *The Blackboard Jungle* were no nearer being answered and, in any event, by the end of the decade the juvenile delinquent was only one of many social and political problems. As a symbol of an alienated society, the teenager might just as well be a werewolf.

caught!

that pure orange flavor...

Naturally, "POPSICLE", the king of all cooling refreshments,
is available in a host of other delicious flavors, too!
You'll find them wherever good ice cream is sold...

...in bags with Polka Dots that youngsters save for exciting gifts!

"POPSICLE" is a registered trademark of the JOE LOWE CORPORATION. Copyright 1953, JOE LOWE CORPORATION, N. Y. 1, N. Y.

CHAPTER SIX

'YOU'VE NEVER HAD IT SO GOOD'
THE CONSUMER YEARS

The years between *The Wild One* and *Lost, Lonely and Vicious* had seen a rapid growth in consumerism, not only in America but throughout the Western world. To an extent, America was seen as the blueprint for the Consumer Society and, as mentioned before, the West recognized with certain misgivings that many features of American society would eventually appear abroad. The cult of the teenager was one of the most obvious manifestations, music being an easily assimilated example of Americanism. By 1958, over 70% of records in America were bought by teenagers. Although the teenage market was valuable, it was seen as having a further and greater importance, which was the conditioning of the young into being consumers. Certain aspects of this worried some contemporary commentators – the introduction of junior credit cards and the targeting of pre-teen girls in particular.

Left *Children were courted as the consumers of the future.*

Below *The bike-riding junior of today is the car buyer of tomorrow.*

Summertime Cottons
by Catalina

For sum
nothing
more "f
a Catali
These gl
swimsui
hips, di
the wais
your bus
rounded

Remem
Catalina
to go sw
keep the
radiant c

Left to rig
Coolie, $1
Gingerbre
Gingerbre
towel, $3-
Sun Stick:
Sun Stick:
Moss Rose
Everglaze

© Catalina,
Los Angele
a division of
Julius KAY
hosiery · lin

Tan with TA

Left *1955 beachwear, which, with greater affluence and leisure became a major part of the fashion industry. Planned obsolescence, of which the consumers were willing victims, demanded that each new look was heavily promoted, only to be arbitrarily dropped in in favour of its successor.*

Right *The stylish 1957 Motorola portable record player was typical of the plethora of items designed to appeal to young consumers.*

Children became prime targets for marketing; by the end of the decade toy sales were worth a billion and a half dollars a year. Moreover, mothers were complaining that their domestic shopping was vetted by their children who were being brainwashed into brand preferences through television advertising. Not only were children a valuable channel through which manufacturers could reach adults, they were also future consumers, and as such were being cultivated for the rich pickings they would eventually provide. It could not have been forseen that the age in which these children ripened into consumers, the sixties, would be characterized by a rejection of consumerism. And so, with a population prediction in 1957 forecasting 60 million more consumers within the next 19 years, they represented a rich potential harvest. An example of thinking ahead comes from an article in *Cash Box* in 1959, bemoaning the fact that although LP records, which at the time were mainly bought by adults were coming out in stereo, there were few singles for jukebox use: 'record manufacturers seem to be losing sight of the tremendous promotional effect stereo singles can have on the public . . . every teenager is a stone's throw away from becoming a young adult who will want a phonograph (probably stereo) for his own home or apartment.'

New from Motorola

So lucrative was the teenage market that manufacturers couldn't wait for childhood to be over and the real build-up to full adult consumerism to begin. Girls, whose destined future would not only be as consumers of clothes and makeup (nail varnish manufacturers were pushing the idea that up to four changes of shade should occur each day to suit various moods, as well as introducing new fashion colours at least twice a year) but also, as wives and mothers, would hold the key to most domestic spending, were prime targets. Little girls were encouraged to ape their mothers and older sisters with children's cosmetics. Brassière manufacturers in particular

could not wait for nature to take its course. In an age when there was a proliferation of truly outstanding role models (Marilyn Monroe, Jayne Mansfield, Sophie Loren, Gina Lollabrigida, Mamie van Doren and Dagmar, star of TV's *Broadway Open House*, whose figure was responsible for Cadillacs' chrome breasts being known as 'Dagmars'), the pre-teen bra, which the New York editor of *Women* magazine Eugenia Sheppard described as 'a limp white object that looks like a dead rabbit', became a best seller. Even so, some disquiet was voiced when the Barbie doll, the first doll with a figure (or as the New York *Village Voice* put it, 'Boobs in Toyland') appeared in 1959. The pres-

surized growing up to which the young were being subjected had the logical result of a reduction in the age at which they married, thus also bringing forward the cycle of house purchase, furnishings, kitchen equipment, then parenthood and so on . . . .

Left *Led on by the subliminal symbolism of plenty, 1950s America favoured ostentatious voluptuousness in both cars and film goddesses. To the rest of the world, this seemed the embodiment of American excess.*

Right *Film and TV stars were constantly to be seen endorsing a range of products with varying degrees of appropriateness. All contributed to the fantasy world of conspicuous consumption.*

Marilyn Monroe

discovers the world's most glamorous
make-up... from the

WESTMORES of HOLLYWOOD

MARILYN MONROE
is now starring in
"NIAGARA"
a 20th Century Fox Production
Color by Technicolor

You can share the wizardry of the world's
foremost beauty experts, the men who make
the stars more beautiful: Perc Westmore, the
dean of Hollywood make-up artists; Wally
Westmore, Make-up Director, Paramount
Studios; Frank Westmore, famous Hollywood make-up stylist; Bud Westmore, Make-
up Director, Universal Studios.

The world's most glamorous stars asked for
it...an *easier-to-apply, longer-lasting* make-
up that would give them the same complexion
glamor on the street that they have in close-
ups on the screen!

And the Westmores gave it to them...fabu-
lous *liquid* TRU-GLO! A make-up that literally flows on your cheek.

You just dot it on, blend evenly with your
fingertips, and pat off excess with a tissue.
Presto! Your complexion takes on a luminous
freshness—a petal-softness—that lasts all day!

Tru-Glo hides tattle-tale lines and imperfec-
tions...draws a sheer veil of color over blem-
ishes...gives you a truly *poreless* look! Even
more important, it imparts a radiant natural
glow that brings out your true beauty!

And...satiny Tru-Glo never streaks. Never
leaves a "masky" look. Not greasy or drying.
The world's most glamorous make-up, magical
Tru-Glo gives you breath-taking loveliness!

*Perfect for all types of skin. Comes in shades to suit
every skin tone. Tru-Glo is available wherever good
cosmetics are sold.*

Acclaimed by Hollywood

Tru-Glo

LIQUID   MAKE-UP

ONLY 59¢ plus tax

(slightly higher in Canada)

Tru-Glo
LIQUID MAKE-UP
Westmore

*Now...a new creamy, smearproof
lipstick...by the Westmores!*

The perfect accent to a Tru-Glo
complexion—Hollywood Lipstick
by the Westmores! And Hollywood loves it because of its in-
toxicating color richness and
exciting sheen...and because it
won't smear. Feels wonderfully
creamy on the lips. Non-drying.

ONLY 59¢ and 29¢ plus tax

(slightly higher in Canada)

WESTMORE *Hollywood* COSMETICS

77

By 1960 the average spending power of the American teenager amounted to four hundred dollars a year. Some one and a half million cars were owned by teenage drivers, and this itself had a knock-on effect: the drive-in movie had first appeared in the late forties and quickly spread, and mobility allowed for the development of out-of-town leisure such as bowling alleys and drive-in diners. The fifties American automobile is a monument to its age, and just as examples from the past (the Egyptian pyramids or medieval cathedrals) embody both the culture and technology of their time, so does the car. The analogy is exemplified by an idea promoted in *House and Garden* magazine in 1958: the in-house garage. In the style of the open-plan living in vogue at the time, it was proposed that the car could be brought into the home, surrounded by house plants and furniture, thus incorporating the garage into the living area. The idea of the home having a shrine to the automobile did not catch on, but by this time the car was already losing its special position, in part because the boom economy of the Eisenhower years was already played out, but also because many Americans were disillusioned with the carousel of planned obsolscence and pressure marketing.

Even the most car-fixated American family probably realised that exhaust fumes would be a major drawback to House and Gardens *proposed in-house garage.*

The drive-in movie is one of the most evocative images of fifties America, combining the magic ingredients of Hollywood, cars, popcorn, coca-cola, and sex.

Nothing dramatizes the gulf between American and European consumerism quite as much as the car. Whilst some American high school kids could drive to school in their own car (itself an integral part of teen culture) only a minority of European blue-collar workers even owned one. Although it had been the car through which Henry Ford had pioneered mass-production, and which through its availability had been responsible for far-reaching social changes (pre-war women found it gave them greater freedom, though their daughters complained that the mobility the advertisers promised them was not such a blessing as they chauffeured the children to little league baseball or brownie meetings and their husbands to the commuter train station in the two-tone monster station wagon which was the mandatory second car) its main function in the fifties was as the pace-setter of planned obsolescence. Other consumer goods followed the automobile industry's example, so that even as basic an item as the refrigerator was marketed as though it were a car, successive models introducing often spurious styling changes and even, at one stage, featuring two-tone paint-work. So much was the automobile industry the essence of the consumer society that even the National Association of Home Builders took it as a model, recommending that anything other than a newly built house should be described as 'used', thus putting it on the same downmarket level as a used car. With the exception of Raymond Loewy, designers saw car styling as an exercise in planned obsolescence. In 1955 the designer Harley Earl had explained, 'Our big job is to hasten obsolescence. In 1934 the average car ownership span was five years; now it is two years. When it is one year we will have a perfect score.'

Left *The Willys Company, which had been saved from oblivion by their famous wartime jeep, brought out a station wagon, seen on this 1950 ad. Its utilitarian functionalism was soon made obsolete by stylish station wagons which often served as the housewife's work-horse.*

Right *Having temporarily exhausted the number of new features with which to woo their customers, Westinghouse brought out the two-tone refrigerator in 1956. Surprisingly, the public were not enthusiastic about this borrowing from car design.*

"It didn't *seem* like 400 miles"

WILLYS *makes sense*

–IN DESIGN   –IN ECONOMY   –IN USEFULNESS

Only Westinghouse Refrigerators

It's like money in the bank! Even when you're not using it, nice to know it's there . . . this surge of

extra **Power**

CORONET V-EIGHT CLUB COUPE

In the new 140-h.p. Red Ram V-Eight engine, Dodge engineers have provided you with a magnificent reserve of acceleration and performance. You take to the highway with greater confidence, greater safety.

And with this surging Red Ram power, you enjoy nimble change-of-pace of new Gyro-Torque Drive. A new road-hugging, curve-holding ride. A new sense of driving mastery.

If your active life demands an Action Car . . . this sleek, trim Dodge is for you. "Road Test" it . . . soon.

Specifications and equipment subject to change without notice.

New-All New
'53 Dodge

The Action Car For Active Americans

Left *This '53 Dodge ad is typical in its blatant exploitation of the power image American car manufacturers acquired through production car racing.*

Right *Hot rodding became a national sport. The car shown in this 1957 picture has lost most of its family saloon origins to become a powerful racing machine.*

Not only were the American designers working in a market whose ideal was conspicuous consumption and where, in comparison with Europe, fuel was cheap, they also had the advantage of an industrial philosophy which could cope with constant retooling at the dictates of marketing. Even the engines were developed under different circumstances. Whereas European family saloons were designed for modest motoring, and only the lithe forms of the elite, sporting Ferraris, Alpha Romeos and Jaguars were seen on the circuit of Le Mans, Detroit's products, featuring massive engines, were entered, both for publicity and development purposes, into N.A.S.C.A.R. Daytona and the Mexican Road Race. Although these 'Stock' cars were made in only small quantities to satisfy the requirements that only production cars could enter, the romantic image of power under the hood was an important marketing factor for the American family car, though this power was coupled with such features as automatic transmission, power steering, power assisted braking as well as comfortable seating and interiors, radios and ever-increasing areas of glass, which gave a car the quality of being an extension of the home.

Design attitudes were represented by two opposing camps. Raymond Loewy championed rationality, with studies in engineering, aerodynamics and ergonomics, coupled with restrained aesthetics interpreted via the designer Robert Bouke into the elegant, European-looking Studebakers. Loewy's motto was 'weight is the enemy', which he took every opportunity to demonstrate, including customizing a Cadillac for his own use, in the course of which the car shed some hundred and fifty pounds of extraneous chrome and decoration.

OLDSmobility

A new mode in motion that takes you out of the ordinary into the Rocket Age!

Cadillac

First Love of 20,000,000 Motorists!

Surveys indicate that there are more than 20,000,000 motorists in America who would rather own a Cadillac than any other motor car built in the land. This is doubtless the greatest endorsement ever given an automobile—if not the greatest ever received by *any* manufactured product. But we think you will agree, once you have visited our showroom, that it is an endorsement richly deserved. The 1953 Cadillac is supremely beautiful . . . its interiors are gracious and luxurious almost beyond description . . . and when it comes to performance—well, this is by far the greatest "Standard of the World" ever built. If you are among the millions who hold Cadillac as your "first love," better stop in and see us to-day. One look and one ride—and we think you will agree that this is the perfect year to make your motor car dreams come true!

YOUR CADILLAC DEALER

The mainstream of auto styling, however, was in the hands of Virgil Exner, Bill Mitchell, Harley Earl and George Walker. Walker was known as 'the Cellini of Chrome' and, with a background as a women's fashion designer, he emphasized Ford's appeal to women. This did not necessarily mean that the cars were designed for women drivers, but rather that the styling took note of the role of the woman in influencing the purchaser's choice. Harley Earl's stated design philosophy was 'Go all the way and then back off', although there seems little evidence of much backing off in the styles of the 'Jukeboxes on wheels' (as Loewy described them) or as *Life* magazine put it the 'high-powered dreamboat that looked as if it had been rolled in chromium batter'.

The automobile industry never achieved Harley Earl's goal of a new model each year. By 1956 the normal body style change came every three years, interspaced with mainly cosmetic changes, and in 1957 this was moving towards a two-year cycle. Variety was further achieved by a vast array of optional extras, to the point where only a small proportion were sold in the basic standard model. Although for 1958 General Motors (Chevrolet, Pontiac, Oldsmobile, Buick and Cadillac) were hoping to re-style each model completely every year, in the event this was achieved mainly by interchanging standard mouldings. By then the public was already disenchanted with the extremes of planned obsolescence.

As the ultimate status symbol the car, whose rapidly changing styles ensured rapid obsolescence, became the icon of the consumer society.

THE BIG M FOR 1958—SPORTS-CAR SPIRIT WITH LIMOUSINE RIDE

Notwithstanding the criticisms of Raymond Loewy, even a design purist is probably obliged to admit the dynamic power which, despite the excesses, characterized late-fifties American car styling.

Too Hot to Hold 'Til '57!

Nash Announces A Completely New Concept in Fine Cars...
New **Ambassador Special** with Torque-Flo V-8...
World's Newest, Most Advanced Automobile Engine

"Compact outside so it's easier to handle and park"

"More room inside than all highest-priced cars"

"Best V-8 gas mileage in its class, Mobilgas Economy Run"

MANEUVERABLE 117¾" WHEELBASE

PRODUCT OF AMERICAN MOTORS

SEE AND DRIVE this completely new idea in fine cars today. So different it makes all the old yardsticks of performance and value out of date.

• All-New Torque-Flo V-8—rifle acceleration, with far more gas mileage than other V-8's!

• New Flashaway Hydra-Matic Drive—whip-quick response, silk-smooth getaway.

• Biggest, most comfortable room ever built into an

• Twice as strong, twice as safe with single unit construction. Frame is a steel, box-girder enclosure as big as the car itself, giving "wrap-around" protection in front, rear, above, below, at sides.

• Completely new riding comfort with bigger, softer springs—world's finest travel car!

• Tops in resale value, because it stays new longer.

Hurry! See this *newest* of all the 1956 cars . . . dis-

SEE THE NEW
Ambassador Special
AT YOUR
Nash

Stylistically, certain elements had now been taken to the limit. The pursuit of size, for example, meant that cars were impractically long for the now congested roads; a Chicago official estimated that returning to pre-war lengths would produce another eight hundred miles of street parking in the city. Ostentation and the pursuit of status were less important now as features of consumerism. As Herbert Bream noted in 1958, the demand was now for 'a new kind of styling, one that will not be an obvious badge of wealth and social importance'. Bream saw in the growing number of European cars being imported a further example of 'the growing US taste for foreign foods, clothes and decor. American tastes and appreciation are widening in cars as well as in other things.' So intense had been the American's identification with the automobile during the fifties that those words can be read as the requiem of that era.

Neither economically nor socially could the pace of change continue. As early as 1957 an article in *Advertising Age* had commented on the publicity for that year's Buick (a notably undistinguished model), which used the word 'new' twenty times: 'We feel it difficult to assume that such complete and utter nonsense is justified by the need to sell seven million cars in 1957. If our national prosperity is to be founded on such fanciful, fairyland stuff as this, how real and tangible can our prosperity be?'

Left *This 1956 ad for Nash concentrates on the all-important power factor. Even so, with its low lines, pillarless roof, large glass area, continental spare wheel and whitewashed tyres it exemplifies all the ingredients of contemporary styling.*

Anglia 2-door sedan, **$1561***, Prefect 4-door sedan, **$1661***

IT'S IMPORTED! IT'S FORD! IT'S YOURS FOR $1 A DAY!

Your trade-in may fully cover the down payment that starts you on the $1-a-day plan offered by most English Ford Line dealers. Applies to the Anglia, Prefect and Escort models.

● **Imagine—a factory-fresh sedan for $1561*** with terms as low as $1 a day! That's just the start of your savings with the English Ford Line. You get up to 35 miles per gallon of *regular* gas. The engine holds only *two* quarts of oil. And you will save on insurance, depreciation, tires, service, registration fee.

You see fine British craftsmanship everywhere in these smart cars. And the name *Ford* assures you of a car that's designed to meet the needs of today's American motorist. That's important, because imported economy cars often omit quality features Americans take for granted.

Take a detail like suspended pedals. They are more comfortable to work, keep out icy drafts, road dust, water. Yet, of all leading economy imports, only the English Ford Line offers this modern and desirable improvement.

Only 150 inches long, the Anglia makes driving fun, parking a picnic. Yet it seats four adults comfortably. And it gives you almost 50% *more* luggage space than either of the other two best-selling imports.

Power?—Compared to the other two best-selling imports, the Anglia has 36% more net horsepower than one; 20% more than the other.

You get almost 2 square feet more visibility in English Ford Line cars than the other two leading imports. *Curved* windshield and rear window.

Service everywhere. The English Ford Line uses U.S. size nuts, bolts, and other fittings. Tools in

any service station will fit. Most imports require special metric-size tools.

Locate your nearest dealer in a jiffy . . . Call Western Union—then ask for *Operator 25*. She can give you the name of your nearest English Ford Line dealer at once. Call any time. How about *now*?

● ● ●

Manufacturer's suggested retail price at Eastern and Gulf ports of entry plus state and local taxes and transportation from P.O.E. White sidewall tires optional at extra cost. Made in England for Ford Motor Company, Dearborn, Michigan, and sold and serviced in the United States by its selected dealers. For further information, write: Imported Car Sales, Ford Motor Company, 3000 Schaefer Road, Dearborn, Michigan.

English **FORD** Line

ANGLIA
PREFECT
ESCORT
CONSUL
ZEPHYR
ZODIAC
THAMES VANS

Above *Incongruous though they may have looked, small British Fords were marketed in the USA. This advertisement appeared in 1959 by when there was a notable public revulsion at the excesses of American cars and an increased acceptance of European moderation.*

The American Dream was becoming tarnished; even President Eisenhower, the champion of consumerism, commented that the people were becoming disenchanted with 'some of the items that had been chucked down their throat'. By now, however, American consumer culture had been extensively exported, with television proving to be as powerful a marketing medium abroad as it was at home. As global television expanded, America became the main source for ready-made programmes. English speaking nations not requiring the expense of overdubbing could buy American programmes at only a fraction of the cost of home production; both Australia and Canada became substantially Americanized in the fifties as a result. Britain, with a longer-established television industry, was less vulnerable, though the BBC bought a certain number of American programmes, including *The Lone Ranger*, *Wells Fargo*, *I Love Lucy*, the *Phil Silvers Show* (Sergeant Bilko) as well as

adopting the format of panel games. The establishment of British commercial television in 1955 not only provided a further outlet for American programmes but more significantly, introduced American marketing techniques to Britain. As neither television nor radio had featured advertising until then, British advertisers had to rely on American expertise. It was even suggested that the London branch of J Walter Thompson had undertaken the research and devised the strategy to ensure the success of the British Parliament's pro-commercial lobby.

In any event, American advertising agencies accompanied the global spread of television (in 1958 J. Walter Thompson had thirty-four branches worldwide), as did American consumer products.

Below *As Britain became a television society it found itself vulnerable to the unsubtle effects of American cultural imperialism.*

Right *Pictured in 1955, Phil Silvers as the scheming Sgt. Bilko found an international audience when his shows became one of American TV's most popular exports.*

The export of American television programmes did have an unforseen effect. Due to the high cost of dubbing for foreign language markets, action stories (Western, police and detective) where dialogue was secondary to the action became prolific. Westerns were particularly favoured due to a high action to dialogue ratio and low production costs. Much of a television western was in fact footage from old Hollywood films; at the time it was said, 'when you see more than two characters, it's stock footage'. The first major TV Western (or horse opera) was *Cheyenne*, each episode of which could be produced in under a week. Its success set off a veritable stampede, with *Maverick, Sugarfoot, Colt '45, Lawman, Wells Fargo, Wyatt Earp, Gun-*

The strapless bra was an essential item in the wardrobe of the fifties woman.

MILLION DOLLAR HOLD-UP!

smoke, *Have Gun Will Travel*, *Wagon Train*, *Restless Gun* and in all a total of thirty different Westerns filling prime time by 1958. *Gunsmoke* topped the ratings, taking 38.8% of viewers.

Not only toy makers but the manufacturers of real guns welcomed this phenomenon; one estimated that having owned on an average fifteen to twenty toy guns in childhood a boy would have been conditioned towards eventually buying the real thing. Nevertheless, the suggestion was fre-quently made that television violence was a major factor in the growth of anti-social behaviour. In the following decade the *New York Times* published a letter on the subject: 'The shooting of President Kennedy was the normal method of dealing with an opponent as taught by countless television pro-grammes. The tragedy is one of the re-sults of the corruption of people's minds and hearts by the violence of commercial television.'

Enjoying a new lease of life on TV after having been a successful radio programme, the Lone Ranger, like other TV heroes, was marketed to young consumers.

Left *President Nasser of Egypt became the champion of Arab nationalism. Both at home and abroad the crisis over Suez (above) was seen as proof that Britain's days as an important power were over.* **Below** *In 1955 Britain faced demands for self-determination from Cyprus, led by Archbishop Makarios, whilst on its doorstep Irish independence re-surfaced as an issue.*

Britain was particularly receptive to the influence of America, which, though resisted by many, was seen as a liberating force in a nation which was only just becoming a consumer society. From the mid fifties ownership of consumer durables such as refrigerators, washing machines and cars increased dramatically, prompting Prime Minister Harold Macmillan's 1957 comment, 'Let us be frank about it. Most of our people have never had it so good.' Although the economy was basicaly weak with a continuing balance of payments problem, the novelty of relatively increased consumer prosperity compared with the years of austerity began a social transformation which was to make its full impact in the next decade.

In many ways the fifties saw the emergence of a new Britain. Physically an extensive programme of re-building necessitated by wartime devastation changed the face of the cities and, together with the creation of New Towns – Stevenage, Harlow, Basildon and Crawley – emphasized a break with the past.

Britain's position in NATO and its atomic capacity kept it a major force in international affairs, although its credibility was severely underminded by the Suez Crisis of 1956. The main social changes which occurred were the dramatic increase in the number of working women, the emergence of an unprecedented youth culture and, from the mid fifties, the arrival of West Indian Immigrants. Popular culture straddled an uneasy line between middle-of-the-road entertainment (much television, for example, was simply re-vamped radio, with performers whose background was either wartime ITMA or even music hall) and the glamour of American television and music. Until its monopoly was broken by commercial television, the BBC had a stultifying effect on pop culture. It ran three channels, one of which was designated as light entertainment, to

which the Corporation adopted a generally patronizing attitude. Rock 'n' roll received little airplay as an arrangement with the Musicians' Union restricted the number of records that could be played, with the result that of the little rock 'n' roll that was to be heard a high proportion was a ghastly parody performed by British light orchestral musicians. Other restrictions took their toll: Chuck Berry's 'Mabellene' was banned as it mentioned Cadillac and Ford by name — according to the BBC this constituted advertising, strictly prohibited in their charter; Gene Vincent's 'Women Love' was banned as too sexy, though in all fairness it was not only banned in parts of America but had also earned Vincent a conviction for public lewdness and

obscenity in the Virginia State Court. The BBC's attitude to rock 'n' roll was echoed in the general condemnation by British Establishment figures; the influential conductor Sir Malcolm Sargent dismissed it as 'nothing more than an exhibition of primitive tom-tom thumping'. The only alternatives to the BBC were Radio Luxembourg, whose powerful transmitters broadcast six hours a night in English over Europe, the American Forces Network and Voice of America. A small number of blues and R&B records were also imported, and it is said that a reason for Liverpool's eventual pre-eminence in British rock was its assimilation of American music through the records brought back to the port by sailors on the transatlantic services. (Although

Teddy Boys featured prominently in the 1958 Notting Hill riots, an explosion of violence against Britain's growing West Indian immigrant population.

the general impression is that the Liverpool sound of the sixties was the first time British pop music had made an impact on America, the short-lived British skiffle craze produced Lonnie Donegan's hit 'Rock Island Line' which reached number ten in the American charts of 1956).

The negative attitude which the BBC and the Establishment adopted towards rock 'n' roll made fears that it would encourage juvenile delinquency a self-fulfilling prophecy. The first generation of British youth to experience a degree of freedom and affluence (by the end of the decade the average teenage weekly wage was £8 a week for boys, £6 for girls, amounting to a total youth consumer spending power of some £850 million per annum) was constantly under suspicion from a society which was still class ridden and socially oppressive. The class element added an extra dimension to the generation gap, which in itself saw tensions between parents conditioned to low or non-existent levels of consumerism and their children with high disposable incomes. The element of violence, which predated rock 'n' roll, had a subliminal effect on the older generation's attitude to teenagers. The images of Dirk Bogarde's *The Blue Lamp* (1950) and the real events of the Craig-Bentley case gave the generation a reputation for being dangerous – an image which some young men were happy to adopt in their body language. *Vogue* magazine commented that 'when people of the older generation see a boy in sharp clothes with his hand in his pocket, they are apt to suppose he is reaching for his flick knife' though this is followed by the explanation that 'in fact he is more likely to be digging out the price of a record or a Coke'.

British police assure an armed Notting Hill resident that she is protected from the rioters. The famous Notting Hill Carnival was set up as a multiracial event in the wake of the riot.

Although jeans arrived in Britain in 1955, Americanism had little influence on the British teenager other than in music. Rather than adopting American style, British youths had their own dress code which combined the forties American zoot suit with an Edwardian look – originally a transitory fashion for upper-class young Guards officers in the wake of the kitsch retro style which had emerged during the Festival of Britain. Into this were incorporated elements of the Western gambler gunfighter such as the bootlace tie and brocade vest. Whilst their girls modelled themselves on American style, the 'teddy boy' was a uniquely British phenomenon.

Unlike its American counterpart, the British teenage scene was not a car culture. Although car ownership had increased dramatically cars were both expensive and, with the exception of sports cars and a few American-styled examples like the Ford Zephyr-Zodiacs or the Austin Metropolitan, devoid of 'image'. The BBC's practice of banning records which mentioned cars by make resulted in some American songs being re-written for the British market, so that Johnny Bond's 'Hot Rod Lincoln' emerged as 'Hot Rod Jalopy' and the Playmates' 'Beep Beep' featured a bubble car rather than a Nash Convertible. There were other incidental differences between American rock 'n' roll as heard in Britain and the American version. Early Fats Domino songs in America were recorded slightly too fast so his voice sounded less 'black' in order to make them more acceptable, though this didn't stop Pat Boone making a career from white cover-versions. For the British market, Fats' voice sounds as it should.

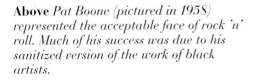

Above *Pat Boone (pictured in 1958) represented the acceptable face of rock 'n' roll. Much of his success was due to his sanitized version of the work of black artists.*

*Christopher Craig (**far left**) and Derek Bentley (**left**) became notorious as young killers. Although it was 16-year-old Craig who did the shooting, it was Bentley who went to the gallows.*

Above *Whilst only the sharp dresser in the middle truly satisfies the strict sartorial criteria, Britain's youth were quickly dubbed 'Teddy Boys' on the slightest pretext by the contemporary press.*

*Heading towards his doom on Route 101.
This 1955 picture publicized Vaughan
Monroe's 'Black Denim Trousers and
Motorcycle Boots'.*

The nearest cultural equivalent to the car was the motorbike. Britain at the time had a world-wide reputation for its motorbike industry and for its performance machines. These became central to an alternative youth scene – that of the bikers or 'ton-up boys' ('ton' meaning 100 m.p.h. doing a ton or over was an integral feature of the cult). Machinery, speed, and the thrill of chicken runs (a test of nerves in which the bikers would deliberately court disaster, the one who held out the longest before taking evasive action being the winner), as well as favouring the harder edge of rock 'n' roll – Gene Vincent, Vince Taylor, Eddie Cochrane – gave them a closer-knit and more classic image than the Teddy Boys, most of whom faded out with changing fashions, leaving the 'rockers' who favoured biker style even if they were not always actual bikers as custodians of rock 'n' roll. At the same time a contrasting movement was beginning which in the next decade would emerge in the form of the 'mods', ideological enemies of the rockers. In the sixties this conflict would result in physical violence, but for the moment they were worlds apart.

When British motorbikes were world-famous performance machines, the 'Ton-up Boys' enjoyed romantic status as dangerous mavericks of the road.

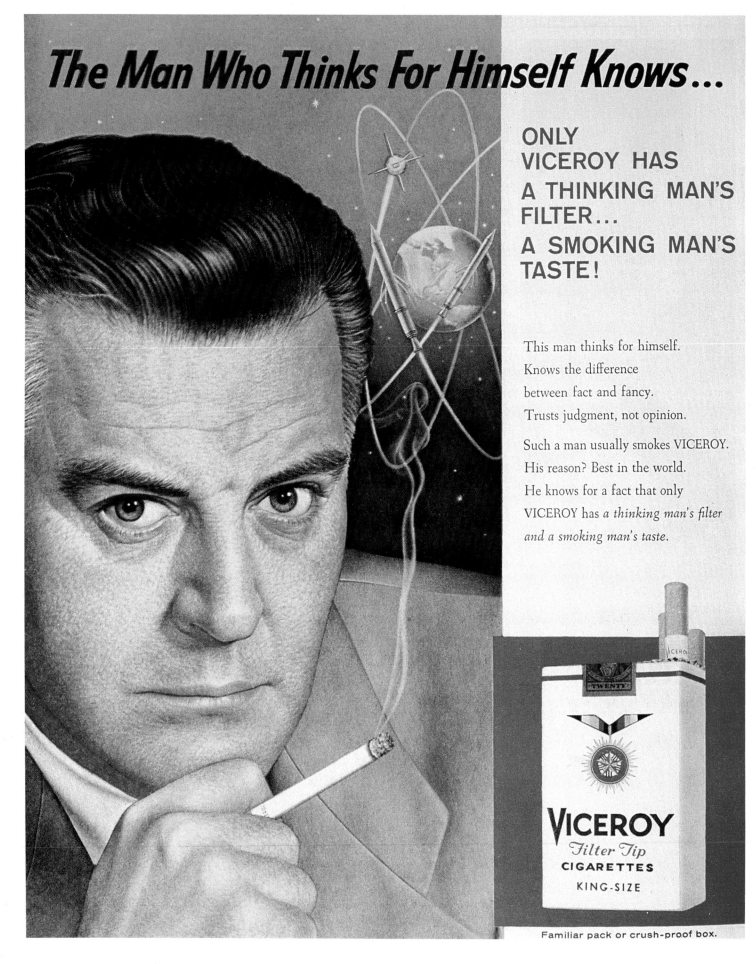

The Man Who Thinks For Himself Knows...

ONLY VICEROY HAS A THINKING MAN'S FILTER... A SMOKING MAN'S TASTE!

This man thinks for himself.
Knows the difference
between fact and fancy.
Trusts judgment, not opinion.

Such a man usually smokes VICEROY.
His reason? Best in the world.
He knows for a fact that only
VICEROY has *a thinking man's filter*
and a smoking man's taste.

VICEROY
Filter Tip
CIGARETTES
KING-SIZE

Familiar pack or crush-proof box.

CHAPTER SEVEN

INTO THE SIXTIES

Left *The Space Race provided many themes for advertisers, as in this 1958 cigarette ad.*

Below *Again from 1958, a surreal flight of fancy advertising Fisher, the automobile body manufacturer. Although space was topical, consumers were actually less interested in the influence of technology than they had been at the beginning of the decade.*

From perhaps as early as 1956 – and certainly by 1958 – Britain and America were set on opposing paths, in that as consumerism increased in Britain it began to decline in its country of origin. In 1955 America had begun the second wave of the cultural imperialism that had been a by-product of the Marshall Plan, with the International Co-operation Administration, which was set up to bolster non-communist countries by, in effect, subsidising their economies and at the same time establishing foreign markets for American consumer goods.

Already the American way of life was being promoted with a crusading zea-lousness. Not only was America involved abroad politically – in the over-throw of Premier Mohammed Mossadeq of Iran in 1953, of President Jacobo Arbenz Guzman of Guatemala in 1954, and in massive financial aid to Ngo Dinh Diem in Vietnam – but was also, through the CIA, using firstly radio and later television as well, carrying out a propaganda war. The U.S. Information Agency (USIA), for example, was in control of The Voice of America from 1953, carrying out the 'ring plan' by which relay transmitters broadcast programmes into Russia, not only encircling Russia with what were essentially propaganda transmissions

but also, by using bands very close to Russian domestic ones, ensuring maximal reception. As, later, Khrushchev was to tell Nehru, "We feel like a beseiged people". To consolidate its position with friendly nations, the USIA supplied free 'information' or 'cultural' films, which were always biased towards the fight against communism. Another powerful propaganda machine, the Armed Forces Television Service, controlled some twenty television and two hundred radio stations, whilst amongst those stations now held to have been directly CIA controlled were Radio Free Europe, Radio Free Asia and Radio Liberty.

In view of this propaganda machine it is obvious that the spread of Americanism cannot be solely attributed to the appeal of Coca-Cola, Wrigley, Marilyn Monroe, Elvis Presley and General Motors. It raises a question mark over the activities of the International Co-operation Administration which by the mid fifties was sponsoring leading industrial design consultants to assist third world countries in establishing viable home industries. There was also a scheme which gave students from those countries opportunities to study in America. Americanism was also promoted via the post-war regeneration of European industry through the European Productivity Agency, which had been established in 1953 by the Organisation for European Economic Co-operation. Europe was generally receptive to this process; Charlotte Blauensteiner of the Austrian Design Institute was typical in commenting how they "started with envious admiration; there was a rich, even affluent society, and of course everybody wanted to have things looking as those from the States". Many aspects of American involvement with foreign industrial regeneration, particularly in the third world, had the effect not only of promoting American political, economic and cultural ideals, but also bonding the relationships by means of an umbilical link of raw materials and service consumables. This 'tied' aid made these countries dependent on America for the continuing supply of essential spare parts and consumables, thus ensuring their continued political allegiance as well as subsidising the aid through these captive markets.

Right *In 1950 this G.M. ad epitomized the 'cultural imperialism' of America abroad. By the end of the decade this had become eroded as the doctrine of conspicuous consumption played itself out and imported European goods began to threaten the home market.*

Below *Agricultural equipment was a major American contribution to Third World economies. Altruism was less of a factor than the desire to keep Communism at bay.*

familiar and trusted part of the rich, full life Americans know. And this is so, very largely, because General Motors men have never ceased trying to improve on their best, have never flagged in their zeal to build better cars each year than they built the year before.

Because of their practiced skill in Research, Engineering and Production, the key to a General Motors car is recognized today as the key to greater value. It is perhaps not too much to say that it is likewise the key to a rich and satisfying life.

GENERAL MOTORS

CHEVROLET · PONTIAC · OLDSMOBILE · BUICK · CADILLAC
BODY BY FISHER · GMC TRUCK & COACH

Krushchev's American visit showed his innate political skill at handling the press. He spent much of his time affably repudiating his bogey-man image.

Despite these ambitious programmes, America's victory in the cold war was not assured. Russia actively participated in international trade fairs, despite having little to offer in the way of consumer goods. Khrushchev, representing the new face of post-Stalin Russia, had embarked on a method of discrediting American political propaganda by presenting an image of a non-aggressive competition between ideologies, thus removing the element of fear which America had been exploiting. In 1957, Khrushchev and Bulgarin made an eight-day visit to Britain, during which Khrushchev promoted tolerance: "You do not like communism, we do not like capitalism. There is only one way out – peaceful co-existence." As part of this programme of shrugging off the bogey man image, Khrushchev masterfully exploited the very medium which America had monopolized as a propaganda vehicle: television. In 1957 he agreed to be interviewed in Moscow by one *New York Herald-Tribune* and two CBS journalists for the CBS TV *Face the Nation* programme, during which he explained that it was America, not Russia which was the aggressor in the cold war, and that although there could be no compromise between their ideologies, the two systems could be in peaceful competition through trade.

Right *Through the International Co-operation Administration the American Government sponsored several educational trips by industrial designers to Third World countries, for instance Russel Wright's visit to Vietnam in 1956.*

The designer as economic diplomat

The government applies the designer's approach to problems of international trade.

Russel Wright, far-flung designer, disembarking on the banks of the Mekong (Vietnam).

Had the dread of communism, which had dominated America since the forties, been without foundation? Ordinary citizens were beginning to question the image of Russia on which they had been fed. Until then, the fear that the ghost of McCarthyism still inspired had limited subversive thoughts to the beat poets. *America*, a satire on American anti-Russian paranoia, (*right*) was published in *Howl and Other Poems*, and resulted in Ginsberg being charged with obscenity in 1957. The case was dismissed, the judge describing *Howl* as having 'redeeming social importance', whilst the local press reported the police seizure of copies of the poems under the headline 'San Francisco Cops don't want no Renaissance', a reference to the literary 'beat' movement, centered on Lawrence Ferlinghetti's City Lights bookshop, that was being heralded as the San Francisco Renaissance.

America it's them bad Russians.
Them Russians them Russians and them Chinamen. And them Russians.
The Russia wants to eat us alive. The Russia's power mad. She want to take our cars from out our garages.
Her wants to grab Chicago. Her needs a Red Reader's Digest. Her wants our auto plants in Siberia. Him big bureaucracy running our filling stations.
That no good. Ugh. Him make Indians learn read. Him need big black niggers. Hah. Her make us all work sixteen hours a day. Help.
America this is quite serious.
America this is the impression I get from looking in the television set.

From *America* by Allen Ginsberg

Above *Often accompanied by modern jazz, poetry readings were an important aspect of the beat movement. Some, like Gregory Corso – famous for such obtuse sayings as 'Fried shoes. Like it means* nothing. Don't shoot the Warthog' – *made much use of body language to enhance their readings.*
Right *The patrons of beatnik coffee bars affected an introspective 'gone' manner.*

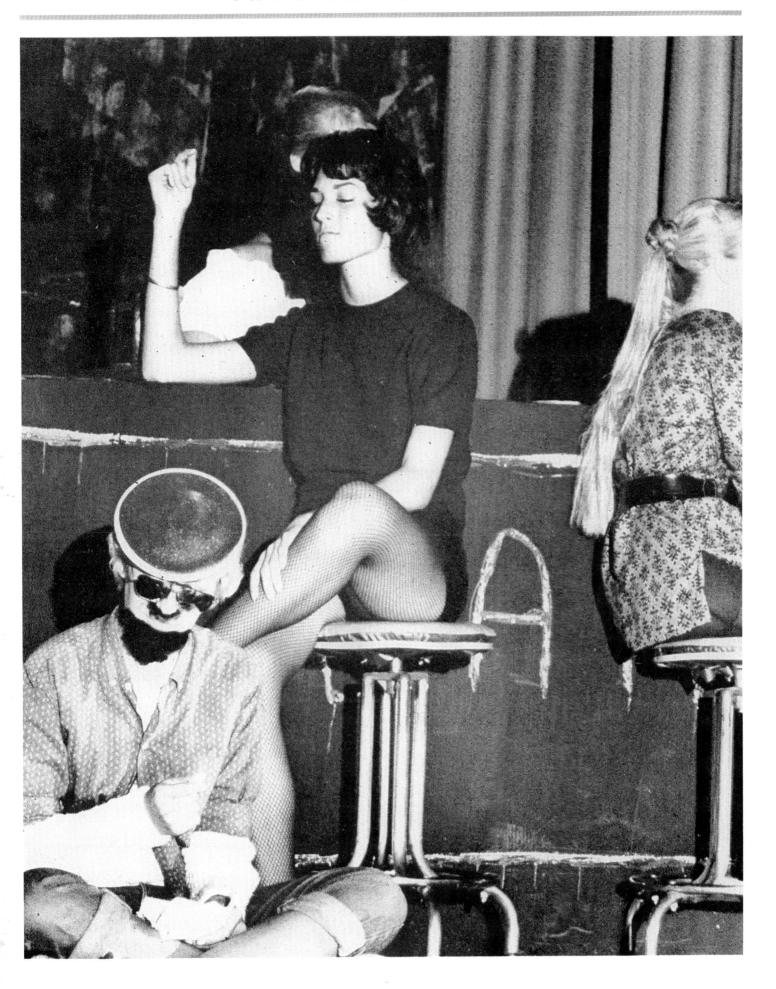

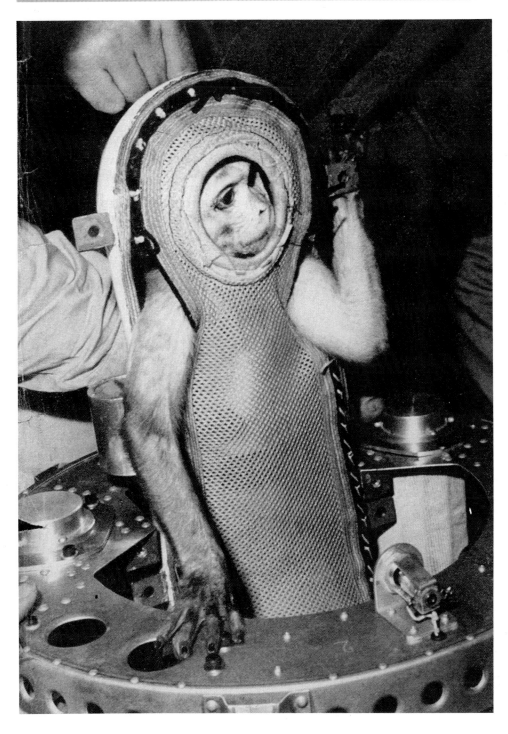

Left *Lieutenant-Colonel John Glenn testing the controls of the American Mercury space capsule, 1959.*

Above *Sam the monkey was the first to test the Mercury capsule, making a thirteen-minute round trip fifty-five miles into the upper atmosphere in 1959.*

On 4 October 1957 Russia astounded the world by putting Sputnik 1, the first satellite, in orbit, encircling the earth at a height of 500 miles at a speed of 18,000 miles per hour. A month later, this feat was surpassed by Sputnik 2, which carried a dog called Laika, the first step in Russia's exploration of space travel.

America had now been effectively upstaged in its main claim to world supremacy – its technology. In December 1957 its first attempt to launch a satellite failed when it blew up on launching. On 1 February 1958 the first American satellite, Explorer, which was miniscule compared with Sputnik 2, was successfully put into orbit.

The whole issue of the validity of the cold war was now being questioned. In Britain, the Campaign for Nuclear Disarmament was formed, representing the opposition to the arms race which was being voiced not only in Britain but also in Europe generally.

In March 1958 Khrushchev ousted Bulgarin as Prime Minister, thus becoming the sole leader of Russia; now the Iron Curtain was to become the open curtain. Although Khrushchev and Bulgarin had begun a programme of foreign visits (the 'K and B Act', as it was known at the time), Eisenhower, who was himself apparently worried that America's industrial-military complex was becoming a Frankenstein's monster, and now deprived of the services of the Machiavellian Secretary of State, John Foster Dulles, (who had instigated the CIA dirty tricks style of American foreign policy and who was now effectively out of the game through ill-health) had no choice but to recognize that Khrushchev was calling the shots. In April the Brussels World Fair, whose theme was peace through atomic power, produced a public reversal of the roles played by Russia and America during the cold war. The Russia pavilion featured as its main attraction the Sputnik. In contrast, the Americans presented a relaxation of propaganda, including one section entitled 'Unfinished Business' which featured problems the nation was now confronting, including racial inequality, urban deprivation, pollution and the threat of depleting natural resources — in fact, the dark side of the glittering American Dream.

In the wake of the Brussels exhibition, America and Russia agreed in September 1958 that the next summer would see an exchange exhibition of cultural technology. Congress allocated three million dollars for this venture, which was to be supplemented by major contributions from participating industries. A Buckminster geodesic dome housed the information centre, which featured a computerised system through which four thousand questions and answers on American life were displayed on a screen, as well as a slide show depicting America in two thousand photos. A second building housed a display of five thousand American products, including an RCA colour television set, a Grand Union supermarket stocked with all the goods which a typical American supermarket would be offering and a typical American kitchen with the latest domestic appliances.

The Russian pavilion at the 1958 Brussels World Fair featured 25-foot statues of a worker and a peasant woman as well as a massive statue of Lenin. Against this background, the Sputnik illustrated the country's technological capabilities.

America was represented by Vice President Richard Nixon who, as an anti-communist hard-liner, could be relied on to ensure that the conciliatory nature of the exhibition (Industrial Design magazine commented that the emphasis on presenting an authentic picture of America had resulted in 'an almost wearying emphasis on credibility, on avoiding the air of propaganda') would not be seen as a recognition of communism.

It had been agreed, in the spirit of the open curtain, that neither America nor Russia would in any way censor televised coverage of the exhibition. Khrushchev was vulnerable to being seen as representing a backward nation being treated to glimpses of American affluence and technology. With the television camera rolling, Khrushchev appeared to be trapped in the kitchen display, which in ways represented the heart of American consumerism; as Erik Barnow described it in *Tube of Plenty*, he 'clearly did not relish the role in which he wsa being cast – a mute country bumpkin listening to explanations from the centre of progress and civilization.'

Edward Stone's design for the US Pavilion, in dramatic contrast to Russia's display of heavy-handed propaganda, exemplified America's presentation of itself as successful culture which could nevertheless admit to having social problems.

Although Nixon was to deny that he had manipulated Khrushchev into the confrontation that became known as the 'kitchen debate', home viewers saw Khrushchev, ill at ease and aggressive, wagging his finger at Nixon who was robustly standing up to him. Despite Nixon's denial, the *New York Times* writer William Safaire has claimed that both the confrontation and its setting had been contrived. The substance of the kitchen debate had been Khrushchev's insistence that kitchen appliances were neither a novelty nor of much interest to Russia, which was fast catching up in the manufacture of consumer goods, and that the public meeting could be better used to discuss the political relationship, most particularly America's aggressive military policy, with its rocket bases all over the world. Nixon, however, was insistent that consumerism should remain the topic: 'Isn't it better to talk about the relative merits of washing machines than the relative strength of rockets?'

The episode had achieved Nixon's goal. For television viewers he appeared, surrounded by familiar domestic appliances, to champion American values. What the viewers did not see was the immediate aftermath. With the debate apparently over, the cameras moved on. During this brief, unrecorded interlude, Khrushchev (who was famous for his ability to switch righteous anger on and off when appropriate) became affable and pointing to the equipment commented, 'This is probably always out of order'. Nixon, aware that Khrushchev would know that the American consumer was becoming increasingly disenchanted with the unreliability and poor quality of domestic appliances (a natural result of planned obsolescence) and secure that this was off the record, jovially agreed.

Although their off-camera dealings are reported to have been amicable, the famous kitchen debate between Nixon and Khrushchev (right) found both leaders ensuring that their home audiences saw them defending their ideologies.

Left *Week after week Van Doren put on a convincingly intense performance which did nothing to betray his advance knowledge of the questions.*

Above *Before a grand jury Van Doren faced questions of a different kind to those of the rigged quiz games which had made him, for a time, a cult hero and role model.*

Between the Moscow exhibition and the reciprocal Russian visit to America, further proof that the Americans' consumer-based society had inherent problems came with the revelation that the popular TV quiz show *Twenty-One* was rigged. Americans were appalled to learn that Charles Van Doren, who had become a cult figure as in show after show, brows furrowed in concentration, he had come up with the right answers, was actually a fraud, having been primed in advance with the questions and answers. By the time he was exposed, Van Doren had won $129,000 and an audience estimated at twenty-five million viewers. Educationalists and church leaders had held him as an ideal role model for the nation's youth – the perfect hero to offer an alternative to rock 'n' roll and delinquency.

In 1959 a grand jury investigation revealed that the rigging of quiz shows by commercial sponsors in *Twenty-One* was typical. The producers of *The Sixty-Four Thousand Dollar Question* and *The Sixty-Four Thousand Dollar Challenge* explained to the grand jury that the sponsors, Revlon, would dictate to them which contestants were proving popular and should be promoted and which had to be dropped, such control only being possible by fixing the game. As the investigation progressed, it became obvious that the quiz games were essentially fraudulent.

Whilst this was going on, a fresh scandal further eroded the credibility of commercial morality when several major figures in the pop music world, including Alan Freed and Dick Clark, host of the *American Bandstand* television show, were accused of accepting bribes to promote records. Although the House of Representatives committee enquiry into the 'payola' scandal exonerated Clark, the nation was astounded to learn of the power Clark had in the industry, and his influence on the young. *American Bandstand* had a regular audience of twenty million viewers, earning Clark, who could make or break a performer, half a million dollars a year. It was claimed that Connie Francis, Bobby Darin and Fabian were amongst those whose success was due to Clark's patronage. A record company executive estimated that simply by playing a record once a day for a week Clark had the power to boost sales by at least a quarter of a million. It was also revealed that Clark's pop music activities extended beyond the *Bandstand*. He also owned a record-pressing factory, a music publishing company and a management company.

Left *Bobby Darin, Frankie Avalon and Pat Boone were amongst the pop stars who paid homage to Dick Clark at his televised 29th birthday party.*

Right *Alan Freed 'Mr Rock 'n' Roll', even had a film named after his title, endorsing his claim to be father of the music.*

Below *American Bandstand produced its own cult stars from out of the studio audience; regulars like Kenny Rossi and Justin Corelli even had their own fan clubs.*

Left *The Pioneer space rocket on the launchpad, 1958.*

Above *Children at school were in the front line of the integration programme. This 1957 picture shows fifteen-year-old Dorothy Counts, whose father was a theology professor, stoically enduring racist taunts.*

The America that Khrushchev visited in September 1959 could no longer claim moral superiority. Worse still, it was now losing its position as the most technologically advanced nation, for, with perfect timing, a Russian spacecraft Lunik 2 had made a successful moon landing, even depositing the Russian flag on the moon's surface only three days before Khrushchev's visit. The previous month, violence had returned to Little Rock, scene of the 1957 de-segregationist confrontation. There was now no aspect of a decade of conspicuous consumerism which could be held up as evidence of superiority.

PAINTED FOR PLYMOUTH BY NORMAN ROCKWELL

"Merry Christmas, Grandma...we came in our new PLYMOUTH!"

The disadvantage from which his hosts were suffering gave Khrushchev the confidence to turn every opportunity to his advantage. Intently scrutinised by the media, he won admiration for his adroit exploitation of television opportunities, effectively becoming a media star. Whatever advantages Nixon may have gained by putting one over on Khrushchev in the kitchen debate were now reversed as he demonstrated his ability to counter American propaganda. In a classic example of his ability, Khrushchev topped an account by Spyros Skouras of how America as the land of opportunity was illustrated by the fact that although he had arrived as a poor immigrant he had been able to rise to become head of Twentieth Century Fox, employing ten thousand people. Khrushchev replied that the Soviet system had allowed himself, who had worked as a shepherd boy from infancy until the age of twelve, after which he had laboured in mines and factories, to rise to the position of head of his country, in charge of a hundred million people.

The further opening of the curtain which occurred with Khrushchev's visit resulted in the White House Christmas-time announcement that the new decade would begin with a summit meeting between America, Russia, Britain and France, and that Eisenhower would also visit Russia. With the spirit of international goodwill emerging during the season of goodwill, the fifties ended on a note of optimism.

Opposite *Norman Rockwell's 1950 portrayal of the archetypal American family has the innocence of a vanished age. By the end of the decade, the simplistic doctrine of consumerism was already discredited, and the children of the fifties were poised to reject the values they had been brought up with.*

Below *Very likely stage-managed by Nixon, the American kitchen provided the perfect setting for Khrushchev to be goaded into verbal confrontation.*

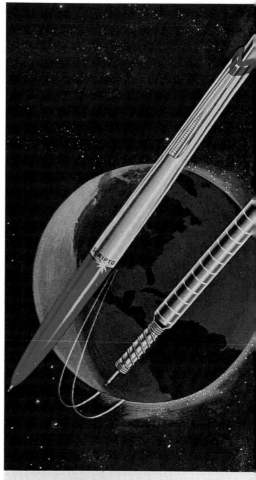

Never before a pen so sli

The stunning Satellite is a masterpiece of
lustrous Satellite metal combined with super-str
Stratosphere blue, Dawn grey, Je

Left *Anticipating the funky sixties, this
Italian monkey jacket was designed by
Capucci in 1958.*

Above *Scripto satellite pens of 1957
capitalized on the topical space theme.*

Right: *Although hot pants were heralded as a new phenomenon when they appeared in the sixties, shorts made a fashion appearance in 1956 and 1957, when they were immortalized in the Royal Teens song 'Short Shorts'.*

Below *Foam furniture, which enjoyed considerable popularity in the new decade, had already appeared in these sixties-looking designs by the Mobay Chemical Co. in 1957.*

and terrific!

. In lightweight,
brilliant Atomic red,
green.

INDEX